Weaving for Worship

Weaving for Worship

HANDWEAVING *for* CHURCHES *and* SYNAGOGUES

by Joyce Harter and Lucy Brusic

1998
Robin and Russ Handweavers, Inc.
McMinnville, Oregon

Robin and Russ, Handweavers, McMinnville, Oregon, 97128
© by Lucy Brusic and Joyce Harter 1998

Printed in Hong Kong by Colorcorp, Inc.

ISBN 1-56659-056-6

Library of Congress Catalogue Number: 97-92738

This book was designed by Lucy Brusic.
All the drawings, except those otherwise credited, were done by Kim Skistad.
The cover was designed by Jennifer Fay of J. Fay Designs.
Portions of the Afterword appeared in another form in *Arts: The Arts in Religious and Theological Studies* 9, no. 1 (1997) and are used here by permission.

Cover: *Easter tapestry* by Denise Mandel for the Basilica of St Louis,
St. Louis, Missouri. Photograph by Marty Keeven.

Ark doors by Laurie dill-Kocher for Congregation B'nai Israel,
Bridgeport, Connecticut. Photograph by the artist.

Robin and Russ Handweavers Inc.
533 North Adams Street
McMinnville, OR 97128-5513
U.S.A.
503-472-5760
FAX 503 472-8220

Contents

Plates

PLATES

Figures and Tables

Publisher's Foreword

I HAVE BEEN WEAVING now for over 51 years—a long, long time. During the course of my years in California, while I was living and teaching in Santa Barbara, I was asked several times to do some weaving for some of the local churches. I looked everywhere for references and found nothing. Ever since that time I have wished for a guide or directory on ecclesiastical weaving.

About three years ago, I inherited some money from my mother's estate. I then contacted Joyce Harter, the author of *Weaving that Sings,* as I knew that she had been doing ecclesiastical weaving for 25 to 30 years before writing her book. I asked her if she would be interested in doing a book on this subject. At first, she was not interested. A year later, I asked again. This time she was receptive, and told me that she would help a good friend, Lucy Brusic, write this book if I would finance the project. They thought it could be done for about the amount of money I had inherited from my mother. I was exhilarated; I honestly felt that my mother would be delighted with what I am doing with my inheritance.

I wanted to cover as wide a scope as possible, so we made the decision to try to cover both Jewish and Christian work. Over a year ago, Joyce and Lucy published calls for work in several weaving magazines. They also sent requests for work to all the liturgical weavers they knew or knew of. Over 150 persons replied; more than two thirds of that number sent pictures of their work. Many wrote to say that they thought such a work was needed and that they could hardly wait to see it.

One of my requirements was that the weaving pictured in the book could be done on 4- or 8-harness looms. With a few exceptions, we have met this goal. A few pieces produced on more complicated looms were so outstanding that we simply had to include them.

Six weavers, in addition to Joyce and Lucy, have contributed the essays in this book. In addition, several others helped with the chapter on commissions. One of our guest authors, Paula Stewart, was one of my students, so I feel that I have a very special contribution to the beginnings of this book.

It is my hope that, with this work as a guide, many handweavers will have the confidence to weave beautiful fabrics for their churches and synagogues.

Russell E. Groff
Publisher and owner of Robin and Russ Handweavers, Inc.
McMinnville, Oregon
August 1997

Preface

MY INVOLVEMENT with ecclesiastical weaving goes back to the 1960s when I was completing a college degree in art education. Weaving classes gave me an opportunity to create projects that would be useful in my husband's field—the ordained ministry. I designed and wove clergy stoles as class projects. Later I found that our friends in the ministry were eager for handwoven work. Eventually, through a friend in the Philadelphia Handweavers Guild, I learned of the work of Theo Moorman. Mastering the technique she developed enabled me to use my ability in graphic design.

Eventually, I developed a small business in liturgical weaving. My work was received at the annual juried weaving exhibits of the Philadelphia guild, including ones that Theo Moorman herself attended.

When we moved to another state I expanded my liturgical weaving business and called myself "Joyce Harter, Weavers." (I felt rather alone in this field. "A *what?*" was usually the answer when my husband introduced me to his friends as "a liturgical weaver.") The business grew as I grew in my ability to answer the needs of small country churches for custom-designed altar, pulpit, and lectern hangings. Clergy were also eager for custom-designed stoles.

I showed my work at regional weaving conferences, but without liturgical weaving as a distinct category the displays were disappointing. To place an altar hanging with table linens, and clergy stoles with clothing, seemed unfair. Nonetheless, these regional meetings gave me a chance to meet other ecclesiastical weavers. I remember a beautiful chasuble woven by Marjorie Ford that was modeled in the style show at a Midwest conference. A chance meeting with her was the first of many friendships with ecclesiastical weavers across the country.

Slowly, articles concerning quality in religious weaving began to appear in weaving magazines, and opportunities to teach about this important form of handweaving arose. Convergence '82 (Seattle) was the first time I taught about my business in this field. Joyce Rettstadt, working on her master's degree concerning the history of the chasuble, was a student in one of my workshops. Since then, we have taught together and she has presented workshops herself. She is the author of the chapter on vestments in this book.

The Toronto Convergence was, I believe, the first to mount a separate exhibit of liturgical work. Since then, liturgical weaving has caught the interest and attention of many more weavers. As the number of weavers interested in this form of weaving has increased, so has the need for help. People have even phoned my studio. I would try to help as much as possible but the conversations would always end with, "I wish someone would write a book about this track of weaving."

This book has taken a circuitous route into existence. After Nadine Sanders and I completed *Weaving that Sings* in 1994, Russ Groff called to compliment us on the quality, but also to challenge me to produce a book on liturgical weaving. I agreed to work on it with Lucy Brusic, who had edited *Weaving that Sings*. We decided that we would like to showcase the weaving of as many people as possible. I gathered names from my extensive list of former students and from many other sources and wrote letters about the book to them. I also advertised for work in various weaving magazines.

Our book became a vital and exciting project because so many weavers and others interested in this field responded to our inquiries. We sent out nearly 250 letters; our editorial board looked at more than 400 slides and photos. Unfortunately, space considerations made it impossible for us to use everyone's work—particularly in categories (or colors) where we had many submissions. Nevertheless, we appreciated the work of so many fine weavers and the time they took to tell us about it. We can certainly say that every thoughtful response helped us refine and define our task and our understanding of weaving for worship.

Joyce Harter
Northfield, Minnesota
August 1997

A footnote on spelling

Relatively common Hebrew words such as *challah* and *matzoh* have been spelled as they appear in Webster's Dictionary; they have not been italicized. *Tallit* and *tzitzit,* although less common, have not been italicized for typographic reasons. Other less common words—such as *kippah, atarah,* and *chuppah*—have been spelled phonetically and italicized after advice from a rabbi. Similarly, the uncommon or foreign names of Roman garments and Eastern Orthodox vestments have also been italicized. All italicized words are defined in the glossary.

Acknowledgements

THIS BOOK HAS come about because of the involvement of many people. One of the most significant to me personally was a weaver who turned down our invitation to write a chapter or even submit pictures of her work, saying that she did not believe that something called "liturgical weaving" should exist apart from any other kind of weaving. She feared that this book would be a "recipe book" for weavers who simply wanted to make things for worship settings. We took her refusal as a challenge. I have kept her letter in front of me, for it helped us decide at the outset that we would not write a how-to manual. Rather we have tried to explain the thought process by which one can design and produce work for worship settings — work that is original, as well as functional.

This personal challenge not withstanding, I owe the greatest debt to the guest authors — all of them professional weavers — who took time from their busy production schedules to write and rewrite chapters for this book. Marjorie Ford was always available to advise me and was especially gracious in helping with the jurying process. Joyce Rettstadt finished her chapter early and patiently answered innumerable e-mail questions. She also introduced me to Marc Hamel and Edward LeSage whose method for constructing liturgical stoles is a substantial part of the third chapter. I spent an afternoon with the three of them discussing the business of liturgical weaving. Paula Stewart took on the task of writing two chapters and answering more questions than she thought were possible about Judaic weaving and Hebrew spelling. Her life is busy in many other ways and I know it was hard to keep refining and defining. Jeanette MacMillan Pruiss was the first to complete her chapter; she gave me the sense and the confidence that the project really could be done. Ina Golub and Steve Medwin, although not writers of complete chapters, supplied substantial material for the chapter on commissions. Ina took the time to comment on two revisions of that chapter. In every case, as I worked with and talked to these individuals I realized that I was meeting a person of deep personal faith, whose spiritual journey is worked out in weaving. In each case, I believe, they see this book, and their contribution to it, as a gift to the next generation of weavers for worship.

Nor would this book have come about without the involvement of my co-author, Joyce Harter. It was she who had the contact with Russ Groff that started the whole venture; she handled all of the correspondence with artists; and she sustained my interest and direction when we were beginning the project. As an author, she, too, wanted to pass on what she had learned, in her business, about liturgical weaving.

Russ Groff, too, is publishing this book out of a personal religious commitment. I am grateful for the time, the interest, and the money that both he and his nephew, Ken Groff, have contributed to this project.

Another group of people who are important to this book are truly too numerous to mention. They are the weavers who sent us photos of their work—many, many more pictures than we could possibly use. Sorting through these pictures was a long job—for us and for our committee—but it helped to shape our thinking. The weavers whose pictures were not used for various reasons, deserve special thanks. They created the work, took the pictures, sent them, and got them back—all without having their name listed anywhere. This is their thank you; their submissions did assure us and Russell Groff that there would be an audience for *Weaving for Worship*. Of course, the book in its final form would not have happened without the artists whose work is displayed on these pages. All sent fine photographs, permitted us to keep them for many months, and wrote intelligent and thoughtful captions. This book truly rests on their commitment and dedication.

Numerous other people must be thanked for individual favors. Fred Gonnerman spent an afternoon taking photographs for us; Lois Malcolm and Ken Kirchenwitz modeled some of the stoles. Brenda Nelson supplied a steam iron and on-site assistance for the photo-shoot. Marie Westerman and Lucille Feroe helped with the photo selection process. Bob Harter bought Ole rolls for my husband on the days when I went to Northfield to work with Joyce. Kim Skistad brought the drawings to me on a rainy night when we both knew she should not be out. Adam Brusic did the black-and-white scans with meticulous attention to detail; he also provided technical support as my computer equipment became more and more complex. Mike Poquette answered numerous questions about the four-color printing process. My brother, William McTeer, supplied legal and practical advice about publishers and contracts.

Jeanne Heifetz forgave me for losing a photograph, and figured out how to supply a replacement.

Rabbi Michele Medwin read the Judaic portion of the manuscript and offered useful comments; she also helped me understand the distinctions between different forms of Judaism. My husband, the Reverend Robert Brusic, read the whole manuscript for clarity, consistency, and ecclesiastical accuracy. He also supported the entire endeavor with patience and forbearance. Don and Barbara Berg, Carolyn Finegan, Lucille Feroe, Mildred Sheie, and Catherine Horn proofread the manuscript at various stages. If, in spite of all their efforts, errors still exist, I, of course, accept responsibility for them.

Lucy Brusic
St. Paul, Minnesota
August 1997

Chapter 1
FABRIC AND FAITH
by Marjorie Ford

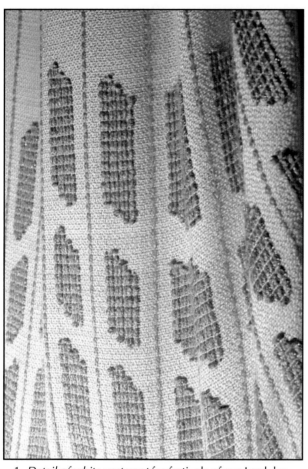

1. *Detail of white vestment* for festivals of our Lord, by Marjorie Ford for Luther College, Decorah, Iowa. 1986. Crepe weave ground with supplementary warp and weft. Warp is 20/2 cotton; weft is 20/2 silk; supplementary warp and weft are metallic and 10/2 silk. As a vestment for high festivals of the Christian year, this detail demonstrates the sensuous richness of fabric. The qualities of flexibility and drape in the piece provide freedom for gesture and movement during the liturgy. The elegant appearance achieved through the use of silk and metallic yarns contributes to the celebratory nature of the Eucharist during Christmas and Easter seasons. (Photograph by the artist)

FABRIC HAS a sensual quality even when stretched flat on a frame. A weaver's hands itch to touch when viewing the sumptuous Italian silks or the intricate Kashmiri wool shawls of a museum's collection. If you are involved in the use of fiber, you may find you have to clasp your hands firmly behind your back to keep from touching. This book is about using that sensual quality to serve a faith community.

As you undertake your new project of weaving a fabric of religious significance, do you wonder, "Why am I doing this?" Some may be creating this project as one in a long series of pieces produced as part of a career in the arts. Another may be trying out this activity for the first time and be somewhat overwhelmed by the implications. Sometimes a friend or family member asks for a prayer shawl at the time of Bar/Bat Mitzvah or for a stole as she/he begins a career of service to a congregation. Perhaps you are the initiator, having a deep religious commitment which aches to be expressed in fiber. However you begin, you are one of a long line of craftspersons and artists who have made significant textiles for religious groups. All these creators started with the background of their culture and a desire to make the very best piece they could to reflect their faith. You, too, start with your own cultural background and your individual personality, desiring to create the best. What can you learn from the past and from other cultures to guide you in your work?

General and ritual uses of textiles

Textiles developed early in the history of humankind and have been in continuous production through the centuries. Earliest discovered were the woven cloths from Catal Huyuk on the Anatolian plateau of Turkey—tiny fragments of plain weave linen dated from 6000 B.C.E. However, impressions in clay from Jarmo, in northeastern Iraq, show that plain weave structures existed as early as 7000 B.C.E.

Cotton fabrics woven as early as 3500 B.C.E. have been found by archaeologists in the Indus River valley. Woven linen produced in Egyptian workshops is documented by a model of a weaving shop from the tomb of Meket-Re, 2000 B.C.E. (now at the Metropolitan Museum of Art, New York).

Since those early times, fabrics have been used to satisfy basic needs: to contain, to clothe, to shelter, and to express. Containers could be basic wrappings or bags or baskets. Clothing existed first to protect human bodies from the elements: later it came to identify groups of persons or to designate a leader. A shelter could be a canopy or a tent or the fabric element of modern architecture. Probably the best conserved textiles are those which result from the need to express emotions—of a group or of an individual. From the placement of a stripe within a Navaho Phase Two chief's blanket to the creation of a complex tapestry series, such as the Unicorn tapestries at the Cluny Museum, Paris, people have told their stories in textiles.

Religious communities use fabrics in symbolic variations of these functions. In Stone Age cultures, precious items were wrapped in fabric to keep them together and to carry them on journeys to new lands. Clothing, which was initially protective, became distinctive. Particular garments identified a whole community, as do the saffron-colored robes of Buddhist monks. Or they differentiated priests, shamans, or holy leaders—as well as secular leaders—from the rest of the community. Not only has fabric been used to cover the living body but also to wrap the body for the next world. The use of shrouds is ancient and continuous. The Ebira-speaking peoples of Nigeria still use a textile with one pattern for wrapping the body of a man and with another pattern for wrapping that of a woman.

The use of cloth to shelter holy places is widespread. Buddhist temples may have banners hanging at the sides of the altar and decorating the enshrined areas. The Moslem prayer rug helps orient the worshiper toward Mecca by indicating the place for head and hands, in another sense of marking the place of worship.

Fabric as a means for telling the story of faith existed in such early sites as a second century B.C.E. temple to Isis in Egyptian Nubia, where portions of large curtains with tapestry iconographic decoration have been discovered. In Angers, France, a magnificent series of fourteenth century tapestries (originally numbering over 90 scenes) tells the story of the Revelation to Saint John.

Origins of ritual fabrics in the Judeo-Christian tradition

This book explores woven pieces that are created for ritual and meditative use within the Jewish and Christian faiths. The creation of Judaic ritual fabrics will be further explored in chapters 6 and 7; this chapter looks only at the distinctive characteristics of their origins. In particular, the fabrics that were used to create the sanctuary and the clothing of the priests were developed from the proclamations of God to Moses in Exodus, starting at chapter 26. The making of the curtains of the tabernacle is described in great detail (verses 1-6):

> Moreover you shall make the tabernacle with ten curtains of fine twined linen, and blue, and purple, and crimson yarns; you shall make them with cherubim skillfully worked into them. The length of each curtain shall be twenty-eight cubits, and the width of each curtain four cubits; all the curtains shall be of the same size. NRSV

The passage goes on to describe the tent over the tabernacle (verses 7-14) and the veil to separate the Holy of Holies from the remaining part of the tabernacle (verses 31-33). In Exodus 28, the vestments for Aaron and his sons, the priests, are described in detail similar to the descriptions of the sanctuary. Later, in Numbers 15, is the directive to Moses for the

2. Mosaic. Church of Sant'Appolinaire Nuovo, Ravenna. Early sixth century. Our knowledge of the shape and decoration of many liturgical fabrics comes from other art forms of the era. Here, we can see in a sixth century mosaic that albs, stoles, and chasubles were in use, as demonstrated by the Pharisee and the Publican illustrated in the scene. Note the "apparels" (rectangular decorative panels) on the robe worn by the man on the left. The drapery in the center may be intended to cover the opening of the Holy of Holies. (Photograph by Charles Pohlmann)

Hebrews to make fringes in the corners of their garments with a thread of blue in the fringe of each corner, in order to remember all the commandments of the Lord.

In contrast to God's explicit instructions to Moses, New Testament comments on the religious use of coverings are symbolic. The apostle Paul writes in Ephesians 6:11, "Put on the whole armor of Christ…" and, in Galatians 3:27, "Baptized into union with him, you have all put on Christ as a garment."

Rather than being based on the Bible, the use of fabrics in Christianity grew out of the culture within which the faith developed. The basic garment, a long tunic, had been worn by Romans of elevated rank or by persons of learn-ing. This garment is the forerunner of the alb (*tunica alba* or white tunic); of the later tunicle, worn by lower orders of clergy; and of the dalmatic, worn by bishops. Another garment, a half-circle of fabric formed into a cone shape, was called a *casula* or little hut, because of its use as a protective cloak. This garment became the chasuble, at first conical, but later modified to other shapes. When the secular culture went on to new styles, church leaders retained the old forms to identify the clergy and to associate them with ecclesiastical tradition.

Emblems of authority from the Roman past were also used to indicate church hierarchy. The *pallium,* at first a rectangular outer garment, later worn folded over the left shoulder as a mark of authority, developed into an insignia of the bishop. This liturgical use can be documented from sixth century mosaics in the churches of Ravenna, Italy. The stole, mark of ordained clergy, developed from this same garment. Another vestment, the maniple, came from a piece of cloth used by Roman consuls to signal the opening of the games and was another indication of rank. In the Catholic church, it became a napkin which covered the left hand when the priest touched the bread of Holy Communion.

Worship practice influenced the development of vestment shapes. Chapter 4 discusses the changes in chasubles in the Middle Ages and in albs during recent times. Following the Reformation, Martin Luther continued to use, on occasion, "mass vestments": chasuble, stole, and maniple. However, he also wore academic clothing, that is, the black robe and sometimes the doctoral hood, during worship. Other reformers wore academic clothing exclusively, signifying their belief in the preeminence of the Scripture over the Sacraments. In an early twentieth century example of borrowing styles from contemporary culture and retaining those garments after they ceased to be everyday wear, the clergy of some conservative Lutheran groups in the United States wore morning suits (formal daytime apparel of cutaway jacket and striped pants) to lead the Sunday services.

In a manner similar to the use of fabric to "shelter" and honor the Hebrew Tabernacle, a Christian church could have canopies over or curtains around the chancel. This practice of "sheltering" the altar or setting it aside as a holy place, is also documented in the sixth century mosaics at Ravenna. These mosaic illustrations of Scripture also show colored silk coverings for the altar to protect the consecrated surface from the touch of the non-believer and white linen covers to catch stray crumbs of the Eucharistic bread. In the Middle Ages, the place of preaching also was marked by a special cloth, at first indicating the academic rank of the preacher. These silk and linen pieces are the beginnings of what became paraments, seasonal sets of colored coverings for the liturgical furniture.

Ritual textiles today

Although Jewish worship today takes place both in the synagogue and in the home, it retains vestiges of the sanctuary fabrics, symbolic shelters, and coverings dictated by God to create a worship space for a nomadic people. The *parokhet* or curtain that separates the ark from the sanctuary, the covering for the reader's desk, and the Torah covers are all developments from the original temple fabrics which designated and sheltered holy places and articles. The same function is performed in Christian churches by a fabric canopy, such as a baldachin, over the altar or a special carpet under it, and by the paraments on some or all of the liturgical furniture. In Jewish homes, a number of fabric pieces are used in the Sabbath meal: challah cover and the Sabbath table cloth. Similarly at the ritual meal of the Christian Eucharist, the vessels which contain the elements are almost universally covered with special—usually linen—cloths: a corporal on which the vessels and elements are arranged, a series of covers for the chalice, napkins for the bread or wafers if they are not presented in a closed container (ciborium).

Clothing the body for ritual leadership also continues. In synagogues, the rabbi and the cantor wear the tallit (prayer shawl); the person who reads from the Torah also wears a prayer shawl. Among Christian clergy, the stole, worn over alb, cassock, or black gown, is generally understood as the mark of ordained clergy. In more liturgical churches, the chasuble is worn at the Eucharist; the cope may be worn at other services; and the dalmatic and deacon's stole may be worn by deacons.

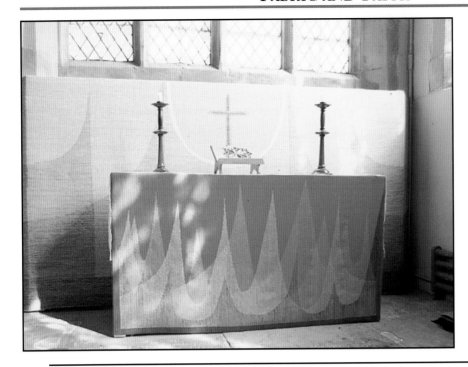

3. *Altar frontal and screen* for the chapel at Coughton Court, Warwickshire, England. Theo Moorman. 1975. (Photograph by Marjorie Ford)

Today the use of fabric as a means of drawing people to worship also means the possibility of other approaches. A piece hanging in an educational facility may teach a story through traditional tapestry technique and pictorial style. A piece in abstract style may foster meditation in a chapel. Contemplate the work of Theo Moorman who wrote that the "weaver is an interpreter, rather than a copier, translating…through knowledge and expertise…"* A three-dimensional fiber sculpture may enhance the spirituality of a worship space. Think of the three tapestries on themes of Creation, Exodus, and Jerusalem which Marc Chagall designed for the reception hall of the Knesset.

The visual elements of color, shape, and texture employed in traditional work are also used in avant-garde pieces. Such pieces—those seen at the Lausanne Biennial, for example, communicate the artist's religious vision without using familiar pictures. A result of this approach is a wide variation in viewers' interpretations—

more so with abstract style than with traditional representation. An abstract composition of color, texture, and structure can create a mood or message which touches people directly and in a very individual way at the place where they hold their sense of the holy. It is possible that the message received is not intentionally conceived by the artist but grows out of the perceptions of both the artist and the viewer.

How to approach a project

Having considered the history of the creation of fabrics for use within religious communities, let us look at their production using the idiom of our own time. First of all, weavers need to remember the essential characteristics of a piece of woven cloth: its primary structure of vertical and horizontal threads; its variable fluidity—from the draping of twills to the firmness of tapestry; its variation in color, fiber, and texture; and its potential for manipulation and for surface embellishment. It is worth noting that a large number of liturgical pieces are rectangular in format, as if the fabric had just come off the loom. Some of the reason behind this characteristic may be owing to the initial use of

Theo Moorman: Her Life and Work as an Artist Weaver, edited by Hilary Diaper (University Gallery: Leeds, 1992) 32.

fabric in this basic form. Ancient garments, such as tunic, toga, and sari were formed by arranging the rectangle. Hangings with square corners fit more naturally into square-cornered buildings. Perhaps a weaver can take a hint from these beginnings, limiting the first creative attempts to the rectangle.

Consider the myriad possibilities. How to choose? A good place to start is by using familiar elements. A wide range of woven structures, fibers, and colors have been employed in the past; no one structure, or fiber, or color is inherently appropriate for use in church or synagogue although some fiber restrictions do occur. For Jewish prayer shawls, linen and wool are not to be combined. Linen for covering the vessels of the Eucharist is preferred in some

Christian denominations. Color systems for festivals and seasons of the church year are followed in the more liturgical Christian churches.

Within these parameters, the weaver can select elements which are known and explore their possibilities. I have used a particular supplementary weft technique for over 30 years, adapting it to the project at hand and experimenting with a variety of ground structures beneath it according to the end use of the piece. Something as simple as balanced plain weave with varicolored stripes, or as complex as the interlacement worked out on a computer-controlled dobby loom, or as individual as a specific approach to color may turn out to be the basis of a body of work.

4. *Parament for Epiphany and the Pentecost season* by Marjorie Ford for Saint John of the Wilderness Episcopal Church, White Bear Lake, Minneapolis. 1990. 30" x 66". Crepe weave ground with supplementary weft. Warp is 20/2 cotton; weft is 2/8 wool; supplementary weft is wool. This altar frontal is part of a set of paraments and vestments created for a neo-Gothic building with a somewhat contemporary, free-standing altar. The amount of stained glass and finely carved ornament and the formal arrangement of the furniture in the chancel suggested a formal design in fine detail in the weaving. The traditional images of wheat, grapes, and growing plants are contemporary in presentation. (Photograph by the artist)

How will the piece be used?

The critical factor is to envision the use of the piece. Does it require the fluidity of a garment responsive to ritual action? Is it a cover gathered up and draped over an artifact or a statue? Is it to hang prominently within a chapel or meditation space where it tells a story and encourages reflection on the subject matter? Will it be carried in procession where its own movement or the forces of the wind will arrange its shape? Will people view it from a distance or from an unusual angle—above, below, sideways, or even from behind? Or will it hang quietly on an altar where its color, texture, and images add to the mood of the liturgy?

Next, consider the people who will use and view the textile. Certainly, a piece created for a children's education space would be very different from that intended for a community's main worship space. Fabric and symbols for a rural congregation familiar with the forces of nature may not be appropriate for an urban community with limited resources for even feeding and housing its members. Another set of choices may be available for a suburban congregation.

The weaver must also be aware that the corporate body of each congregation has a unique belief system. Today in the United States, a range of practices exists among synagogues; among Christian denominations, a variety of beliefs affect worship. It is wise to explore thoroughly the practice and beliefs of the community for which the piece is intended before suggesting something which might be viewed as out-of-date or even inappropriate.

The weaver will also want to consider the characteristics of the space in which the piece is to be used, although the designer need not be a slave to period styling. A neo-Gothic building can have a variety of textiles. The great Gothic cathedrals of Europe themselves incorporate design styles from many periods, in both architecture and decorative elements.

What is needed is sensitivity to the dimensions of the space, the shape of the space, the type of architectural materials and their colors, the scale of structural members and of decorative detail. Avoid the permanent installation of a huge, bold, and gaudy banner that overwhelms the liturgical arrangement of a tiny and intimate room. On the other hand, recognize that a large, elaborately decorated space will require boldness in a new element, for it will need to speak to the people from a distance. Sometimes the incorporation of a contemporary style will serve to update or revitalize a space which had a worn-out look.

The dimension of time is also important. Some fabrics, such as Torah covers, are used repeatedly. Others, such as dossal hangings, are permanently installed. Funeral palls or banners for a particular festival are used only periodically. Occasional use brings up another consideration: storage of these articles. If facilities are limited, the pieces should be simple in shape so that they can be folded (with washed, unbleached muslin or acid-free tissue paper in the folds) and placed in a drawer or hung over a padded rod. A community may want to have the message of its artifacts available even when they are not being used in worship. Arrangements can be made for visible storage on the walls of gathering places, corridors, and/or meeting rooms.

Images and symbols

At this point, it is important to discuss another design concern—the use of graphic images. Historically, pictorial symbols have been widely used by Christianity. On early Coptic tunics, the vertical bands called *clavi* incorporated pictures of saints and stories from scripture. In medieval vestments and paraments, similar illustrations were woven in or embroidered on with great skill. A whole system evolved for identifying persons, events, or theological motifs by a series of images. For example, the dove is a symbol of the Holy Spirit, or an apron full of roses identifies Saint Elizabeth of Hungary. (The roses were transformed from the bread she was distributing to the poor in spite of her husband's disapproval.) These symbols were seen and understood by the wearer and by those in the culture.

Today, these elaborate symbol systems are no longer absolutely necessary, since most people can read the stories of faith. Now the message can be illustrated directly through the elements of color, texture, line, and shape—the vocabulary of visual communication. What is often described as abstract art is the use of these elements in a direct manner rather than combining them in a pictorial representation. In a sense, this activity is reimaging the symbols so as to make them relevant to today's culture. If a weaver is working in this way, it may be helpful to include one or two traditional symbols to provide a point of entry for people who are familiar with the traditional images. It is wise to select carefully; the symbols of one community may have different meaning in another community.

Although some artists create art for the community without themselves being believers, most of the weavers represented in this book create as members of a faith system and are probably most comfortable producing pieces for that community. Likewise, a viewer who knows the cultural tradition and historical iconography of a faith system will more quickly grasp the complex meanings of a ritual piece than will an outsider.

On the other hand, a designer may sometimes find that those who are most familiar with the ritual do not understand the way in which the visual represents the theological content of the ritual. People may know that water is involved in Christian baptism, but not understand why there are three streams on the banner (to symbolize the Triune God in whose names the baptism occurs) or why a cross is included (to reflect the words "...child of God, you have been sealed by the Holy Spirit and marked with the cross of Christ forever," which are part of the baptismal service). Sometimes, a teaching aspect must be combined with the presentation of designs so that the uninitiated or those who are unfamiliar with the iconography will be able to respond to the message being conveyed.

Role of fabrics in worship

The role fabrics play in religious experience can vary. In some cultures, fabrics can be the focus of devotion. Maria del Rosario Pradel, in a paper presented at the 1996 Symposium of the Textile Society of America, described the Tenjukoku Shucho, two embroidered curtains in the Japanese Buddhist Temple at Chuguji. These curtains depict the paradise of Tenjukoku and are worshiped as an icon. These fabrics have gained holy status because of their presence in the temple and because they are a replica of the original curtains. The originals were referred to as a mandala or representation of the cosmos and the replicas are accorded the same reverence.

In Christianity, on the other hand, the role of textiles derives from their usage—as garments, covers, and objects of expressive art—rather than as objects of devotion. (The exception might be a fabric of such importance as the Shroud of Turin.) The napkin covering communion bread indicates that this bread is special. The priest putting on a stole may say a prayer of vocation. In some denominations, the presiding minister vests in the chasuble during the service to illustrate the shift in liturgy from Word to Sacrament. Sometimes churches use fabrics—banners, decorations for a festival, costumes—to create environment, whereas others

5 a, b. *Presence* by Marjorie Ford for the Lutheran Church of Christ the Redeemer, Minneapolis, Minnesota. 1988. Overall dimensions: 9' high x 13' wide x 2" deep. Crossed warp weave (leno) with supplementary weft; warp is painted with dye in darker opaque areas. Warp and weft are 10/2 linen; supplementary weft is wool. The space is very simple and intimate. This simplicity called for a piece to make this environment special, a place of worship. The transparency of the weave structure helps to diminish the solidity of the front wall, create a more open and freeing space, and give a sense of God's mysterious presence. Colors move from dark to light, suggesting light overcoming darkness, and Christ, the light of the world. The message is that God is always present in the life experience of the people. (Photograph by the artist)

use traditional vestments and paraments to symbolize continuity with the early church. Of course there is much overlapping between these two attitudes. Sometimes textiles may *appear* to be the objects of devotion, whereas they are actually acting as images to enhance prayer and to mark the *place* of devotion. Small woven images for the Stations of the Cross or a tapestry of Biblical subject matter behind the altar are examples of such a use.

In Judaism, fabrics play similar roles in worship. Torah covers protect and honor the scroll. A chuppah provides shelter over the marrying couple as indication of the family life begun at marriage. There is also a range of practice, varying among orthodox, conservative, and reformed synagogues. In some cases, the rabbi and the cantor will wear prayer shawls; at others, all men will wear prayer shawls as a sign of faith; in some congregations, women will also wear the garment. Although God forbade the production of graven images, many instances of representational design do exist in synagogues and homes.

Abraham Joshua Heschel writes in *Man's Quest for God* that the distinction between the religious and the non-religious use of decoration lies in understanding the purpose of decoration: "to enhance the love of doing a *mitzvah* (religious act); to add pleasure to obedience, delight to fulfillment. Thus, the purpose achieved is not in direct contemplation but in combining it with a ritual act; the art objects have a religious function but no religious substance."* One way to glorify God is by making or acquiring beautiful objects for the enhancement of worship.

Closing comments and comforts

In Exodus 28 God directs that those who are exceptionally skillful in craftsmanship are to offer their artistic skill for the making of vestments, an instruction to which Jews and Christians of today could respond by using the

gifts of skill and resources of materials they have received. It is important to bring all the knowledge of structures and color theory—all the skill of threading the loom and throwing the shuttle—to bear on the project at hand. If you are at the beginning of a weaving career, you should use the knowledge and skills in which you have confidence. Even then, the creative process contains one additional element. The spiritual journey of the weaver is an integral part of the project and will enrich what is offered. The work is the result not only of technical experience, but also of the life experience of the artist.

Nonetheless, you need not feel overcome by the implications of this new project. The Danish theologian Søren Kierkegaard has written,

> When a woman makes an altar cloth, so far as she is able, she makes every flower as lovely as the graceful flowers of the field, as far as she is able, every star as sparkling as the glistening stars of the night. She withholds nothing, but uses the most precious things she possesses....But when the cloth is finished and put to its sacred use: then she is deeply distressed if someone should make the mistake of looking at her art, instead of at the meaning of the cloth; or make the mistake of looking at a defect, instead of at the meaning of the cloth. For she could not work the sacred meaning into the cloth itself, nor could she sew it on the cloth as though it were one more ornament. This meaning really lies in the beholder and in the beholder's understanding. **

Remember that weavers, like all people, come as students on a journey of faith and as servant creators; perfection is God's role.

---

* Abraham Joshua Heschel, *Man's Quest for God* (New York: Charles Scribner's Sons, 1954) 123.

** Søren Kierkegaard, *Purity of Heart*, rev. ed., tr. Douglas V. Steere (New York: Harper & Brothers, 1948) 27-28.

6 a. *Birkot Hashamayim (Heavenly Blessings)* by Marjorie Ford for Bet Shalom Synagogue, Hopkins, Minnesota. 1988. 11' high x13' wide x7' deep. Lace or mock leno (Bronson) with supplementary warp. Warp and weft are 2/24 wool; supplementary warp is wool. This piece was commissioned by a congregation that had purchased a neo-Gothic church for their synagogue. After remodeling to arrange a place for the ark, eternal light, reading desk, and chairs, the congregation still felt a need for something to identify the site as a place of their own worship.

6 b. *Detail* (above) The piece has a *chuppah* at its center, which is lowered for the wedding ceremony; the individual panels are much like the fabric of a prayer shawl. The circular, billowing forms suggest the clouds of heaven, the protective and encompassing presence of the Lord. The three loops of each section suggest the threefold priestly benediction spoken at the end of each service and also used to bless bride and groom, newborn child, Bar/Bat Mitzvah. The *chuppah* has seven sections which imply the seven benedictions that are part of the wedding ceremony. The use of form and color without naturalistic representation conveys messages which can be interpreted and enlarged on by the personal experience of the worshiping observer. (Photographs by the artist)

7. *"Fountains Abbey Illuminated"* by Sylvia Garfield, North Haven, Connecticut. In the collection of Luther Seminary, St Paul, Minnesota. 1991. 19" x 31". Double weave pick-up with a supplementary warp between the layers. 10/2 cotton. The inspiration for this piece was a visit to Fountains Abbey at night when the abbey ruins were silhouetted by colored illumination. The piece was not woven for a specific site, but rather to study the effect of double weave with black and multiple colors. (Photograph by Fred Gonnerman)

CHAPTER 2
QUALITY,
COLOR, AND SYMBOL
by Lucy Brusic

8. *Sacred Head* by Lucy Brusic. In the collection of Luther Seminary, St. Paul, Minnesota. 1986. 37" x 119". Crackle weave with inlay. Warp is 5/2; weft is wool. This work was inspired by the painting "Crown of Thorns" by Alfred Manessier. All the color changes are in the warp or are laid in; the pattern weft does not vary. The piece is particularly designed to suggest a red cross at a distance and then to draw the viewer closer by small details of laid-in metallic and other bright colors. (Photograph by Fred Gonnerman)

QUALITY, COLOR, and symbol are the building blocks of weaving for worship, though these subjects are not equally covered in the literature. Colors used by communities of worship today are fairly well agreed upon, at least within the liturgical churches. Symbolism as a topic seems to divide weavers into two camps—those who use identifiable symbols and those who prefer to keep symbolism abstract. Quality is almost never mentioned, as though there were no outside standards by which to judge weaving. The purpose of this chapter is to provide some background information on each of these subjects. The remarks pertaining to quality apply to all weavers for worship. Color and symbols for Judaic weavers are covered in chapters 6 and 7.

What does quality mean?

Quality in weaving begins with design. In order for a design to be successful in a religious setting, it must be appropriate—historically, liturgically, and artistically. The historical and liturgical outlines of what is appropriate in Judaic and Christian weaving are discussed in other chapters of this book. What is appropriate artistically is harder to define, but it should certainly include a discussion of the quality of the weaving. Quality in weaving means that selvages are straight; beating is even; yarn joins are invisible; and mistakes (if any) are not obvious. By extension, it means that materials have been properly chosen and correctly handled in warping, weaving, and finishing.

Good weaving begins with a plan. This plan outlines the size and shape of the finished item, or determines the yardage needed to produce it. As in any sewing project, a muslin pattern might even be used to test fit, size, and placement of design. Even though modifications may be made while the piece is being woven—or after it is off the loom—an overall plan is a blueprint for the quality of the completed product.

Materials

When it comes to selecting materials, the best available yarns are the best starting point. Reliability of color and certainty with finishing details are much greater with yarns whose fiber content and properties are known. Moreover, materials from known manufacturers can be reordered. The cost of these materials can be recovered as a tax deduction if the item is to be donated to a church or synagogue.

It makes sense to sample—especially with any new yarn—to make sure that the product drapes or hangs correctly for the intended liturgical use. Many professional weavers simply find a yarn and a technique that work and stay with them, thus avoiding the sampling aspect of weaving. Others continue to experiment throughout their careers.

Marks of quality

- High quality yarns
- Careful weaving
- Straight selvages
- Appropriate color, shape, and size
- Careful finishing
- Straight hems and seams
- No wrinkles
- Durable style and work
- No obvious errors

Once threaded, the warp should be tested and errors, if any, corrected. If you have enough yarn, it is a good idea to wind on an extra yard or so of warp. Errors that are not visible until weaving begins do slip into projects; it is nice to be able to start over again without having to unweave.

The physical qualities of the weaving will be visible for a long time in a worship setting. The beat should be even and the yarn joins classic in their subtlety. Selvages should be straight, although many weavers find that turning a narrow hem along the selvage edge is a good way

to produce a straight side edge. A temple or stretcher is a necessity on a piece of weaving that is supposed to hang square, such as a wall hanging or a table covering The stretcher should be moved forward every inch and a half. Even if a piece of cloth is to be cut and sewed, it will not hang straight if it was not woven squarely.

Simple is best

Simple projects and shapes are the best place to begin. They are easier to visualize and execute and easier to install and keep in shape.

Finishing and construction

Finishing is a key factor in liturgical weaving. Material to be cut and tailored should be washed as appropriate. If material is to be washed in warm water, test the color-fastness of yarns before weaving with them. (Tying two pieces of yarn in a knot, putting them in hot water, and then untying them after they dry will show whether or not a color is fast.)

Tapestry and other hangings have their own finishing techniques. A cold water bath will help soften and relax a fabric that is not designed to be laundered.

Pressing is an essential part of finishing a fabric. Even fabrics that will not be tailored should be carefully steam-pressed and allowed to dry flat or rolled on a tube. It is not an elevating experience for the weaver or the worshiper to sit in a pew and contemplate a wrinkle that could and should have been steamed out.

Hems should be even. Measure the hem of a parament or a stole as though it were a dress hem, from the floor.

Not all weavers are sewers. If the project involves construction, consider employing a seamstress to help with the final details.

Color

The second element in weaving for worship is color. Color is an important part of the drama of the Christian church year and an important part of why weavers in general weave.

The colors of the church year do not have as long a history as do the shapes of vestments. Colors in ancient frescoes vary. White appears frequently, perhaps because dyes were expensive. Innocent III, who became pope in 1198, is the first author to mention a color sequence. He listed red for Pentecost and the days of saints and martyrs, black for Lent and Advent, white for ordinary days before Pentecost, and green for ordinary days after Pentecost. Substitutions were permitted: yellow for green, violet for black, scarlet for red.

However, this system may have been more descriptive than prescriptive, for a lack of color-fast dyes and the general poverty of churches meant that many churches had at most two sets of vestments—a regular set and a festival set—of whatever color. (Vestments were sometimes made from clothing that the wealthy had donated to the church.) A common practice was to wear the newest or most magnificent vestment, ignoring the color, on the highest festivals. This practice is still used in most Eastern Orthodox churches.

COLORS OF THE CHURCH YEAR		
Name of season or day in church year	Color used by Lutherans and Episcopalians	by Roman Catholics
Advent (4 Sundays before Christmas)	Blue	Blue-violet
Christmas to Sunday after Epiphany (January 6)	White	White
Epiphany to Lent	Green	Green
Presentation of our Lord (February 2) and Transfiguration	White	White
Ash Wednesday	Black or Purple	Purple
Lent (40 days before Easter)	Purple	Purple and red-violet
Palm Sunday (if celebrated as Passion Sunday)	Scarlet or dark-red	Scarlet or dark-red
Holy Week: Monday–Wednesday	Scarlet or purple	Purple
Maundy Thursday	Scarlet or white	White
Good Friday	Black or none	Red
Easter (begins during Easter Vigil)–Pentecost	White and/or gold	White and/or gold
Ascension (40 days after Easter)	White	White
Pentecost (50 days after Easter)	Red	Red
Pentecost (also called Trinity) season	Green	Green
All Saints' Day (November 1) and Sunday following	White	White
Christ the King (last Sunday in church year)	White	White or gold
Saints days and other occasions of celebration	Red or white	Red or white
Reformation Day (October 31)	Red (Lutherans only)	
Thanksgiving Day (USA)	White	Green or white

Color in the church year

Today, at the end of the twentieth century and thanks to the liturgical renewal movement, Roman Catholic, Episcopal, and Lutheran churches are for the most part using a common color calendar. The basic colors for the liturgical seasons are white, red, violet, and green—with blue being added by Episcopalians and Lutherans for the season of Advent. Black is used occasionally, but minimally, in some Christian churches.

The color system followed by liturgical churches—and some non-liturgical churches—is as follows:

Blue is the color used for Advent (the four Sundays before Christmas) in the Lutheran and

9. *Clergy stole* by Janet Bealer, Atlanta, Georgia, for Church of the Atonement (Episcopal), Atlanta. 1994. 96" x 4½". Twill and twill damask, warp- and weft-faced plain weave. Warp and weft are silk and merino wool. This is one of a pair of matching stoles used in a small, simply furnished church during the Christmas and Easter seasons. (Photograph by William Culp)

Episcopal churches. *Purple* may also be used for Advent. Although the use of blue in the Roman church was prohibited by papal ban in 1570,* a blue-violet—as distinct from the purple of Lent—is permitted during Advent. *Violet* may be used in Roman Catholic churches for masses for the dead.

White is the appointed color for the season of Christmas and the first Sunday after the Epiphany (January 6). Some churches continue to use white paraments until Lent, although many churches switch to green during Epiphany.

Purple and red-violet are the appointed colors for the Lenten season, the forty days (excluding Sundays) before Easter. On Palm Sunday, the Sunday before Easter, some churches, including Roman Catholic churches, switch to *scarlet* or *dark red*. Roman Catholic churches may also use *red-violet* on the third Sunday of Advent.

White and gold are the colors for Easter. These colors are used for 50 days—from the Easter Vigil until Pentecost, the day of the Holy Spirit. *White and gold* are also used for feasts and commemorations, such as the Transfiguration and the Annunciation. *White* is generally used on All Saints' Day, November 1.

Red is used on Pentecost, saints' days, and other occasions of celebration. Roman Catholic churches use *red* or *scarlet* on Good Friday.

Green is the color for the season of Pentecost, also called Trinity season. This season of growth, hope, and regeneration can last anywhere from 22 to 27 weeks. *Green* is also the color for the season of Epiphany, the time between Christmas and Lent, in many churches.

---

*Blue vestments disappeared from the Catholic church except in Spain where blue may only be used on the feast of the Immaculate Conception or special feasts for Mary.

Some churches use rose, yellow, or off-white for designated periods of the church year. Each denomination, and occasionally a local church, may have its own system of color. It is the weaver's responsibility, whether he or she is being paid or making a gift to a church, to know and respect the color sensibilities of a given worshiping community.

Even though artists must be knowledgeable and sensitive about the use of prescribed colors, room exists for interpreting the season's mood rather than conforming to rigid rules. Thus, using somber grays and muted purples with other drab colors is suitable for penitential periods. Using golds and reds with white to express majesty for high feasts is also encouraged as is a range of greens used with blues and yellows for the long period of Pentecost/Trinity.

10. *Clergy stole* from a chasuble and stole set by Beth Cawkins, Pittsburgh, Pennsylvania. Private collection. 1996. Twill. Cotton. This stole and a matching orphrey for a chasuble were woven from one long warp. The weft was black, but was woven with a 3/1 twill so that the colors would show as much as possible. (Photograph by John M. Cawkins)

Light and color

The interior lighting of churches can do strange things to yarn colors. Reds and whites will remain red and white, but purples that have too much blue will be very dark and greens that look quite green in daylight may become blue under incandescent light. (Perhaps this is the reason that avocado green is so frequently used in churches.) Whatever yarns will be used should be sampled under all potential lighting conditions. Lustrous yarns, such as rayon and silk, that reflect light are often especially effective in dark interiors. Gold gimp in the warp or as an accent in the weft will also help to reflect light.

Symbolism

As noted in the beginning of this chapter, symbolism in religious weaving is a controversial subject. Many practitioners and users of religious weaving say that color and shape are the only symbols that are needed. A clergy stole tells the congregation that the person who is wearing it is a pastor. The color of the stole reflects the liturgical season. A purple chasuble tells the congregation all they need to know about the person who is wearing it: he or she is the presiding minister for a communion service during Lent. These people say that no other symbols are necessary.

Other weavers and worshipers feel strongly that symbols are an important part of the Christian tradition, dating from a time when the images in stained glass windows and stone carvings were the only way that an illiterate congregation could "read" the stories of the church. For these people, a symbol points to and participates in the transcendent.

Both points of view will be covered in the following discussion to show that religious meaning can be conveyed in both realistic and abstract symbolism.

Some common symbols

Many Christian symbols are available. The cross is the most obvious, and it lends itself to many woven structures. Other symbols have evolved through the centuries. A crown of thorns and nails are symbols of the crucifixion. A butterfly and a lily are both symbols of the resurrection. A cup and a plate or a cup and a loaf of bread are symbols of the Eucharist, as are grapevines and sheaves of wheat.

Fish and loaves of bread recall one of Jesus's miracles as well as the apostolic history of the early church. The Greek letters Chi and Rho are symbols for Jesus. A dove is usually a symbol of the Holy Spirit and tongues of flame suggest the Holy Spirit's descent at Pentecost. In more abstract ways, triangles and interlocking circles represent the trinitarian aspect of the Godhead. A hand may symbolize the deity.

Since the variety of symbols available to the Christian weaver is so great, it is unfortunate that some symbols have been so overused that work with them looks old-fashioned. (Ironically, many symbols, even the overused ones, are not understood by members of the laity.) In general, Christian theology is receptive to the idea of new symbols and new representations of theological ideas, so long as the symbol points beyond itself and is consistent with the traditions of the church. If symbolism is desired, necessary, or expected, then the weaver/designer should try to create new symbols worthy of a new piece of weaving. Of course, such new symbols should be dignified, appropriate and capable of theological explanation.

Some artists find it helpful to look at historic uses of symbols, to research their original meanings, and to use this knowledge as a springboard for designing. Looking up all the uses of a word in scripture, using a concordance, can also be a tool for new perceptions .A sound knowledge of church history and theology is an indispensable aid in this task.

Guidelines for working with symbols

- Symbols can be used in thoughtful combinations that have particular, or new, meaning.
- They can be incorporated into weaving if the design work and the execution are done skillfully.
- The transcendent meaning of the symbol, both in its particularity and its generality, should be able to be explained.

11. *Lilies* (detail of pulpit parament) by Bonnie Nelson, Seattle, Washington, for First Covenant Church, Seattle. 1992. 31" x 18". Dukagång. 7/2 wool and metallic. This motif is adapted from the lilies in the leaded glass windows of this church. The parament is one of several sets commissioned by this church. (Photograph by Peggy Washburn)

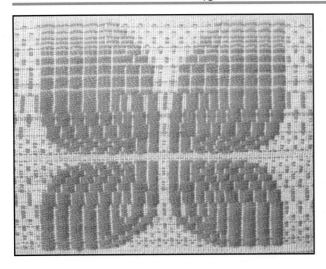

12. *Detail of funeral pall* by Marjorie Ford for Minnehaha United Methodist Church, Minneapolis. 1981. Random warp and plain weave with supplementary warp. Warp is 20/2 linen and 10/2 cotton; weft is 2/8 wool; supplementary warp is wool. The butterfly is a traditional symbol for the Resurrection. It was repeated in two rows on a funeral pall as a symbol of the Christian risen with Christ, represented by a cross at the center of the pall. The pall was woven in lengthwise sections on a 16-harness dobby loom, which made it possible to keep track of the large number of sheds. (Photograph by the artist)

13. *Tree of Life* (detail of pulpit parament) by Sallie Guy, Murray, Kentucky, for Fondren Presbyterian Church, Jackson, Mississippi. 1990. 49½" x 17". Theo Moorman technique. Ground warp is 10/2 cotton; tie-down is 40/3 cotton. The Trinity season coincides with the seasons of renewal and growth in nature and appropriately uses the color green. In parallel fashion, this season also emphasizes renewal and growth in the Christian faith. A tree of life in which the leaves gradually change into crosses reflects this emphasis on a pulpit parament. It coordinates with the matching clergy stoles for this church, which have motifs of a vine, also a symbol of growth. (Photograph by the artist)

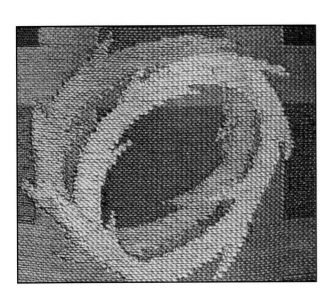

14. *Detail of pulpit hanging* by Joyce Harter for Atonement Lutheran Church, St. Cloud, Minnesota. 1980. Theo Moorman technique. Rayon and linen. The crown of thorns that was placed on the head of Jesus is a central symbol of the season of Lent. The shadow effect of this crown of thorns is an example of how the Moorman technique can be used for pictorial symbolism. A shadow effect makes the symbol more commanding. (Photograph by Neal Olson)

Abstract symbolism

A weaver who does not use symbols in weaving for worship is not restricted to plain weave. Abstract symbolism also has a respected place in liturgical art. Color striations or stripes, both of which are natural to weaving, evoke both mood and thought. Simple laid-in blocks of color are effective in communicating a religious theme. The effect of a warp-designed color progression with a repeating pattern can assist worshipers in meditation.

Non-representational design will sometimes go in the direction of selecting a weave structure that suggests cross forms or other symbolic

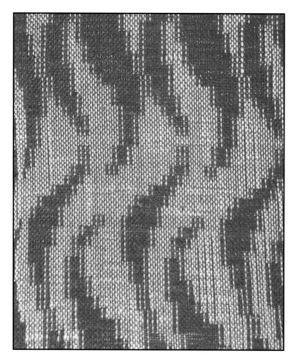

15. *Tessellating Flames.* Detail of Pentecost stole by Christine Spangler, Silver Springs, Maryland. In the collection of the artist. 1996. 188″ x 5½″. Double supplementary tied weave in 14 blocks, with two shafts for the tie-down. Warp and weft are silk. The flames, a symbol of the Holy Spirit, interlock in a vertical tessellation. The pattern is threaded in an advancing twill order; the edge follows a straight threading order. The advancing threading enlarges the pattern and blurs the edges of the design. In the warp, one thick pattern thread alternates with a thin (sewing silk) tie-down end. In the weft a thick pattern pick alternates with a thin tie-down pick. (Photograph by the artist)

16. *Lectern hanging* (sample for parament) by Gulli Kula, Lexington, Massachusetts, for University Lutheran Church, Cambridge, 1995. 25″ x 7″. Star of Bethlehem overshot pattern converted to supplementary warp. Warp and weft are Shetland wool; supplementary warp is heavy silk. This piece was the sample for an altar cloth. The altar cloth was done in two patterned widths and one plain width which were sewn together. The artist chose wool to avoid wrinkling; the piece was lined as is this lectern hanging. (Photograph by Fred Gonnerman)

characters. Crackle and monk's belt are adaptable to cruciform shapes. Other structures can be used with color or texture to produce fabric that is expressive without pictorial content.

Nonetheless, since most people view liturgical weaving from a distance, any design—abstract or not—needs to be large and distinct. The best designs will also possess complexity when viewed close up. If the woven piece is an article of clothing, the design should not interfere with the drape or fit of the garment; simple color changes and repeating patterns can accommodate this need.

In conclusion, the weaver can use colors and symbols in many personal ways to convey religious meaning. However, he or she must remember that weaving for the church, like hymnody or the liturgy, is the servant of worship and ought not to draw attention to itself. If liturgical weaving is to be taken seriously, it must be quality weaving. It must also be correct—historically, liturgically, and artistically.

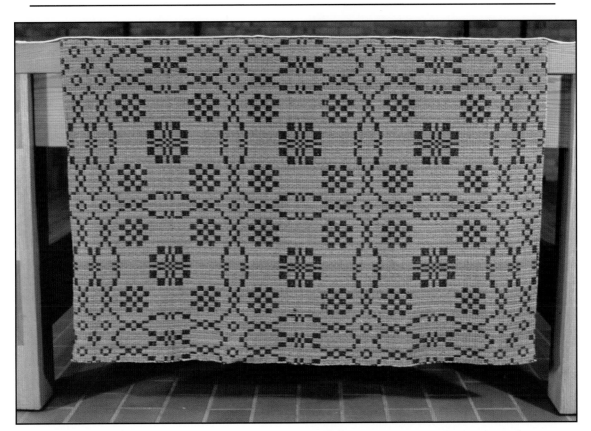

17. *Kingdomtide communion table cover* by Mathilda C. Murphy, Meadville, Pennsylvania, for Garber Memorial United Methodist Church, New Bern, North Carolina. 1994. 35" x 71". Summer and winter (6 shaft, 4 blocks). Warp is 3/2 perle cotton; tabby weft is 5/2 perle cotton; pattern weft is cotton chenille. This communion table cover was the third of a series of commissioned paraments. The sanctuary is a plain, almost spartan space; the center of attention is a large, free-standing wooden communion table. The first two sets were runners with appliquéed symbols; for this set, the congregation requested something that would not be symbolic. The "Methodist Wheel" from *The Shuttle Craft Book of American Hand-Weaving* by Mary M. Atwater suggested itself; it was transferred to six-shaft summer and winter to eliminate long floats. The table cover can be turned 180° ; the other side is a multi-shaded green. The table cover warms the atmosphere of the sanctuary, and the balance of the design is visually restful. (Photograph by Fred Gonnerman)

WEAVE STRUCTURES FOR LITURGICAL WEAVING

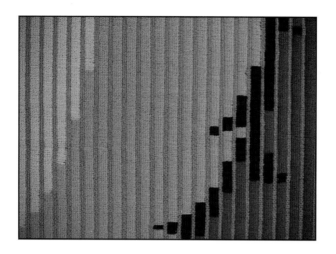

18. *Detail of Lenten parament* by Elaine K. Olson, Eau Claire, Wisconsin, for Luther Seminary, St. Paul, Minnesota. 1986. Overshot. Wool. An overshot threading was used as the base for an interlocking tapestry weave. This piece was woven from the back. A full view of this parament is on page 59. (Photograph by Fred Gonnerman)

19. *Detail of white chasuble* by Evelyn Tuller, Friday Harbor, Washington. In the collection of the artist. 1992. Mary Ann Ostrander overshot pattern. Warp and weft are 2/12 merino wool; pattern weft is Astraglow and metallic. This motif of purple and teal blocks was placed on the front and the back of the chasuble; the blocks are separated by silver weft threads. The pattern was chosen for its resemblance to two overlapping crosses. The rest of the vestment was woven in rosepath blocks on a textured, white ground. (Photograph by the artist)

20. *Detail of chasuble* by Janet Bealer, Atlanta, Georgia, for St. Luke's Episcopal Church, Atlanta. 1992. Twill damask using naturally dyed silk. The fish was chosen as the motif in this positive/negative twill damask pattern in which the "positive" fish and the "negative" fish are "swimming" in opposite directions. The crosses were woven on a separate band which was hand sewed onto the main piece. The chasuble is part of a set of vestments and paraments that incorporate two other patterns of more strictly geometric motifs. (Photograph by Anderson Flewellen)

21. *Detail of clergy stole* by Joyce Harter. 1980. Monk's belt. Rayon and linen. The simple monk's belt pattern with the prominent cross form is a distinctive weave for liturgical work. The pattern can be varied in its layout and used in a number of ways. (Photograph by Neal Olson)

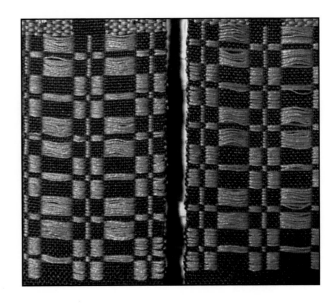

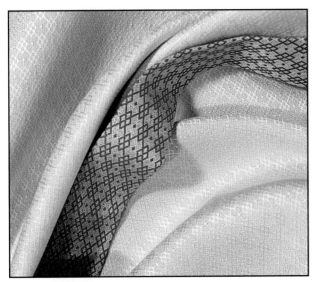

22. *Detail of chasuble orphrey* by Joyce Rettstadt. 1991. Eight-shaft reversing twill. Silk. This orphrey was created on a twill threading by using a doubled weft thread with a Lurex tabby. This resulted in an enlargement of the pattern. The same threading was treadled as a twill to create the fabric for the chasuble shown on page 48. (Photograph by Nash Studio.)

23. *Detail of ikat stole* by Patricia Wronsky, Langeley, Washington. In collection of the artist. 1993. Plain weave with hand-dyed ikat and metallic accents. Warp and weft are merino wool. The ikat stripe was a way to soften the color change between the light and dark purple and add visual continuity to the piece. It was necessary to weave both sides of the stole simultaneously to have the pattern match. (Photograph by Chris Wronsky)

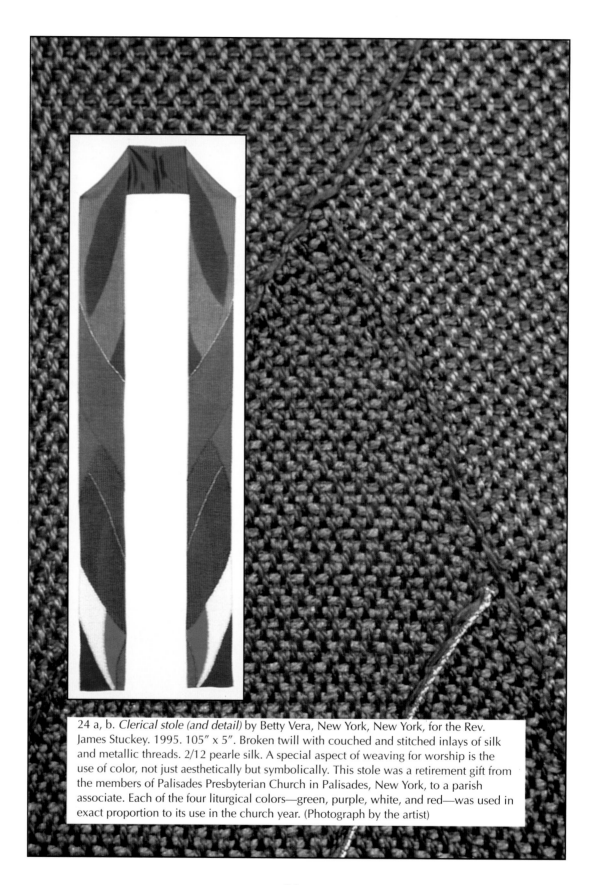

24 a, b. *Clerical stole (and detail)* by Betty Vera, New York, New York, for the Rev. James Stuckey. 1995. 105" x 5". Broken twill with couched and stitched inlays of silk and metallic threads. 2/12 pearle silk. A special aspect of weaving for worship is the use of color, not just aesthetically but symbolically. This stole was a retirement gift from the members of Palisades Presbyterian Church in Palisades, New York, to a parish associate. Each of the four liturgical colors—green, purple, white, and red—was used in exact proportion to its use in the church year. (Photograph by the artist)

Chapter 3
The Liturgical Stole

by Joyce Rettstadt, Marc Hamel,
and Edward LeSage

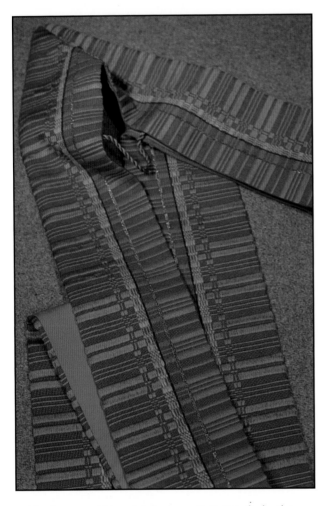

25. *Green and blue stole* by Joyce S. Rettstadt, for the Rev. John Spangler. 1994. 114" x 4½". Turned monk's belt. Cotton and wool. This stole uses blue with "liturgical green"—reflecting the references in texts for the season to water and growth. Turned monk's belt is time-consuming to warp and thread but very fast to weave with a single shuttle. It would be a good weave for multiple stoles. (Photograph by the artist)

THE LITURGICAL OR pastoral stole is the symbol of the ministry in many denominations. Ordination ceremonies usually involve vesting an ordinand with a stole as a symbol of the yoke of Christ. The stole announces to the congregation that the person wearing it is an ordained minister. In many Reformed churches, the stole is the only vestment used—over a preaching gown or an alb.

In churches that observe a liturgical calendar, the color of the stole also announces the season of the church year. On the other hand, some churches and some pastors use an all-purpose stole, incorporating all of the liturgical colors into one design.

In spite of their widespread use and symbolism—or perhaps because of it—stoles have many variations in size, shape, and method of construction. Moreover, fashions change—even in stoles. In the late twentieth century, the stole is frequently worn over an alb and is fairly long, the more so if it will be worn under a chasuble. When pastors wore a cassock and surplice (a black, fitted robe with a loose-fitting outer vestment), stoles were no longer than the surplice. Stoles were even shorter when pastors wore only a preaching gown.

The preferred width of stoles has changed, with the current preference for stoles about four to five inches wide. Even the practice of each clergyperson owning a complete set of stoles has changed, as churches often order stoles to match a set of paraments.

Many weavers begin by weaving a stole as an ordination gift. Even though a stole is a small project which can be done on a narrow loom, it is not a simple project. As an article of clothing, a stole should drape well and move with the wearer. It should hang straight and be comfortable to wear. It should not be showy or distracting, but at the same time, it should '"read" from a distance. At its best, a stole will clearly be custom-designed without shouting that it is handmade.

Stoles as symbols; symbols on stoles

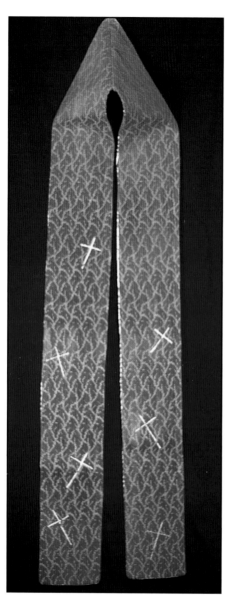

26. *Lenten clergy stole* by Christine Spangler, Silver Spring, Maryland, for Grace Episcopal Church, Washington, D.C. 1990. 120" x 6". Diversified plain weave variation, 16 shafts. Cotton and silk. In this clergy stole, the entwined thorns represent the crown of thorns, and the seven crosses, the seven deadly sins. The warp was hand painted in seven hues of violet and the crosses were embroidered by machine. (Photograph by the artist)

Some writers say that the stole is a symbol in its own right; it does not need added symbolic images. A leading liturgical authority, the Rev. Andrew Ciferni, says that "in virtually all images of vesture from the classical, medieval, and Renaissance periods, vesture is not decorated with images. Breastplates, apparels, orphreys, and the bottoms of stoles are truly structural elements which decorate construction instead of being constructed decorations." *(unpublished letter)*

Meanwhile, another school of thought holds that symbols, if used correctly, are an important aid in directing the eye to the minister and the mind to meditation. If symbols are used, they should be designed so that they fit the stole and can be seen. If the minister or priest does not walk in a procession, or if he/she stands behind an altar or a lectern during the service, then it makes sense to design symbols to be used on the upper portion of the stole. It goes without saying that one should be careful with the placement of symbols on stoles designed for a woman.

If a client wants symbols, consult original sources. Many reference books give pictures of symbols. *An Illustrated Encyclopedia of Traditional Symbols* by J.C. Cooper. is especially recommended. Rather than copying designs from liturgical catalogs, look at Renaissance paintings or early mosaics. Read the Bible. Try to illustrate verbs like *multiply, divide, bypass, eliminate, add, subtract, subdue, invert, extrude, separate, distort, magnify, rotate, diminish, rearrange, flatten, squeeze, alter, adapt, or substitute.* Of course, if you decide to design entirely new symbols, be sure to check with the client.

27 a. *Parament set* for Pentecost by Shannon Eisert, Wenatchee, Washington, for Grace Lutheran Church, Wenatchee. 1993. Stole is 112" x 5½". Lee's Surrender overshot pattern. Warp is 5/1 perle cotton. Weft is same and wool. The artist wanted to create a bold pattern, using rich colors, for her church. She left the altar piece unlined to enhance movement, but lined the stole to improve the way it hangs. The stole needed special care during construction to keep the two sides matching, since it was woven in one piece.

27 b. *Detail* (right). The artist chose colors of red and orange to evoke "tongues of flame" for Pentecost. Two shades of red wool in the weft increased the depth of color in the central blocks. (Photographs by Randy Dawson)

General considerations for the design of clergy stoles

1. *What color is desired? Is this a special occasion stole? Does the wearer have a preference for style, yarn, design, or weave structure?* The answers to these questions may influence decisions about shape and construction.

2. *Will the stole be worn by more than one person?*
   If the stole is to be worn by several ministers, it must be neither too long nor too short for any of the wearers. This assignment may be impossible if one person is 6'6" and another 5'2". In that case, two stoles will be needed.

3. *How wide and how long should the stole be?*
   Although a stole is not a fashion statement, it should be comfortable and attractive. Fashions

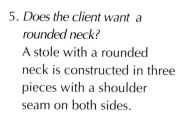

change, but the average-sized stole is currently four to five inches wide and approximately 55 inches from the center back of the neck to the finished end of the stole. The stole should be long enough to hit below mid-calf or show below the hem of a chasuble. It should also go with the chasuble with which it will be worn.

4. *How will the stole be worn?*
   Generally stoles hang straight, but some ministers like to cross the stole over their chest. In this case, it may be necessary to add extra length. Some ministers anchor a stole under the cincture, which may influence the placement of designs.

5. *Will the stole be slightly tapered to neck area, or straight?*
   If the stole is to be worn beneath a chasuble or if it is worn by a large-breasted woman, a tapered shape may be desired. This may be a gentle taper from the hem to the neck or it may

take the form of a gentle curve from the chest area. If the stole is worn under a chasuble, then it should lie flat around the neck area. If, however, it is to be worn over an alb or an academic robe, a straight strip is acceptable.

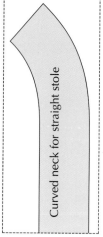

5. *Does the client want a rounded neck?*
   A stole with a rounded neck is constructed in three pieces with a shoulder seam on both sides.

6. *What neck angle is required to make the stole hang straight down?*
   All shoulders are not created equal. If you are having trouble getting the right angle for a client, take long strips of paper the width desired and drape them over the client's shoulders. Allow the strips to hang straight down the front. At the back of the neck, take a straight edge and connect the top and bottom points where the two strips cross each other. That is the proper angle.

7. *Will a neck cord be attached?*
   A neck cord is a decorative rope or small chain attached across the back of a stole to keep the stole from riding forward on the shoulders. The placement of the neck cord can do two things. 1) A cord placed high on the back will keep the stole flat around the neck and shoulder area and keep it from shifting. 2) A shortened neck cord further down the neck will produce a graceful shape resembling a hood at the back of the shoulder area. This stole cannot be worn under a chasuble because it

Reproducible stole patterns are found on pages 137–139.

General considerations...

will form a lump under the garment. If you use a neck cord, you must add extra length to your pattern since the cord will shorten the distance from center of the "V".

8. *Will the stole have fringe or tassels?*
Yardage for either a hem or a fringe must be figured into the length of the warp. Fringes and tassels should be of professional quality. Fringe left at the bottom of handwoven material is very attractive but generally needs yarns added to make it full. Handwoven fringes may also be specially designed and woven. Consider how well these finishes will hold up during successive dry cleanings.

9. *If the stole is lined, will the lining match?*
Sometimes a contrasting lining is attractive. However, a lining may also detract if the stole is very colorful. If you decide to use a lining, take samples of fabric with you to match or to contrast with lining material. Some people prefer cotton or cotton/poly for lining because it does not slide as does satin or polyester lining material.

10. *How will the stole be stored?*
A stole should be stored flat, with padding at any folds. Handwoven fabric will hold its shape better if the stole is not hung on a hanger.

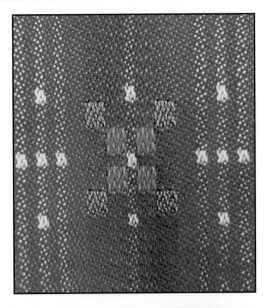

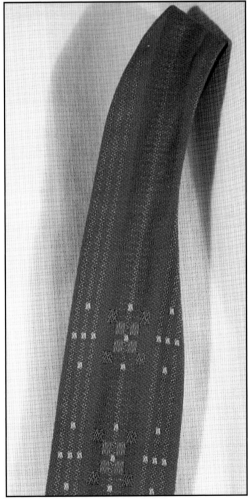

28 a, b. (right) *Pastor's stole for Advent* by Phyllis Waggoner, Golden Valley, Minnesota, for Hennepin Avenue United Methodist Church, Minneapolis. 1992. 112" x 4". 10/2 cotton. Damask on a draw loom. The Gothic style church in which this stole is used is dominated by large stained glass windows. Narrow borders of figures or flowers surround the large main figures in the windows. The artist chose the red rose border in the Nativity window to adorn the pastors' stoles for the Advent season and used the most intense yarn colors she could find. She created her own pattern for the shaped neck by taking apart a worn-out stole. (Photographs by Fred Gonnerman)

THREE WAYS TO CONSTRUCT CLERGY STOLES

Weavers have evolved different methods of weaving stoles for modern liturgical use. Three methods are described in this chapter. The first method is for a lined stole similar to stoles available commercially. These stoles are lined, interlined, and, except for the neck seam, hand-sewn. The second method creates an unlined stole that does not require cutting, lining, or extensive hand finishing. A third method creates self-lined stoles especially suited to loom-controlled patterns.

These directions assume that the weaver has sampled yarns enough to know how to produce the desired weight of fabric and has the sewing skill to construct the stole as described. We also assume that the weaver has studied stoles that are in use in churches to get an idea of correct shape, weight, and feel.

Choosing a weave

Choose a simple weave structure if color combinations are important. If, on the other hand, the texture of the weave is important, then choose an interesting weave and let the color combination be subordinate.

Using handwoven fabric

When you are using handwoven fabric to construct a stole, wash the fabric and press it to be sure that any shrinkage takes place before the stole is completed! You may also wish to preshrink any cotton lining. It is a heartbreak to put a lot of time and effort into a beautiful stole only to have it turn into a wrinkled mess later. Use a lightweight woven, fusible interfacing on the back of any delicate or loose weave. This interfacing will stabilize the fabric and make it easier to handle.

---

1. The lined stole

These stoles are interlined, lined, and finished by hand. The only machine stitching is done at the center back seam. The lining material is often chosen by color suitability, although it should not be a slippery material.

29. *Jerusalem cross stole* by Hamel-LeSage Studio. 1997. 114" x 4–5" wide, tapered. Summer and winter. 2/18 wool/silk. This stole, produced according to the construction method described on the following pages, uses a cotton/poly broadcloth lining. The lining was sewed in after the stole was completed and is inset ¼" from the edge of the foundation fabric. The tassels were hand tied from the warp threads; each knot has exactly eight threads in it. (Photograph by Marc Hamel)

Making a lined stole

As far as the ends of the stole are concerned, three finishes are standard: plain, fringed, and tasseled. These directions are for a stole with plain ends. (If you want to make a stole with a fringe that is part of the handwoven fabric, then eliminate molding the bottom hem in step 19. If you wish to use tassels, sew them on before you make the hem, as in step 13.)

Make two patterns

1. Decide what pattern you are using for your stole. (Patterns appear on pages 137–139.) Using a grid to enlarge the pattern, make two full-sized heavy paper (oak tag/manila paper) patterns. One is for "molding" the foundation fabric and the other one is for "molding" the lining. The lining pattern should be ½-inch narrower than the foundation pattern to allow a ¼-inch margin on each side. The lining pattern should be one inch longer so there is a portion for turning under at the hem. Cut out the patterns and label them. *Remember that the patterns do not include seam allowances.*

Cut foundation fabric

2. Place the larger oak tag pattern on the foundation fabric (right side up), being sure to center the pattern if necessary. Trace a cutting line ¾-inch from the edge of the pattern. (You only have to trace and cut around the sides and bottom of the stole. You will leave about one inch of fabric at the top uncut for the time being.) Cut the fabric. Do this for both halves of the stole.

Mold foundation

3. With the fabric face down, center the pattern on the fabric and use a steam iron to mold first the seam allowance of the bottom and then the seam allowance on the two sides of the stole around the pattern. Leave the seam allowance at the top open. Do this for both halves of the stole.

Overview of stole construction

1. Make two patterns—the foundation and the lining (the lining pattern is ½-inch narrower).

2. Cut two pieces of foundation fabric with seam allowance.

3. Mold foundation.

4. Measure. Cut length at neck edge with seam allowance.

5–8. Sew angle, open, and press.

9–10. Do the same with lining fabric but do not mold at bottom. Leave extra at bottom to fold under.

11. Cut interlining for foundation.

12. Complete foundation by inserting interlining and fastening with Stitch Witchery®.

13. Add optional tassels.

14. Cut interlining for lining. Leave lining interfacing extra long; it can be trimmed later. Glue neck seam of lining interlining together with fusible interfacing.

15–16. Run a line of wide Stitch Witchery® between foundation and lining interlinings. This fastens the two interlinings together.

18–22. Add neck cord if necessary. Place molded lining around interlining. Slip stitch lining to foundation.

Measure

4. Lay the two halves of the stole foundation face to face and mark a cutting line for the neck using the angle at the top of the pattern. *Remember to add seam allowance.* (See remarks about getting the correct angle on page 28.) Pin the stole together below the line and then cut along the line.

Sew angle, open, and press

5. Open the molded seam allowances and pin

the fabric together in each fold and across the angled neck line.

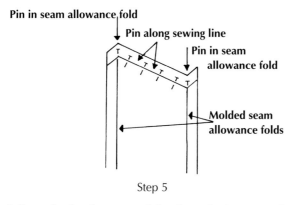

Step 5

6. Sew the back seam of the foundation together following the shape of the cut fabric and leaving a ⅝-inch seam allowance. Mark the fabric with a sewing line, or use the guide plate on the sewing machine. The guide plate on the sewing machine is faster and more accurate.

7. Cut out a notch at the peaked end of the neck and make a small slit at the valley end of the neck, being careful not to cut through the sewing line.

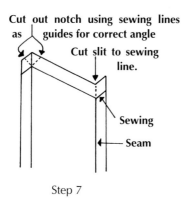

Step 7

8. Press the seam open on the inside.

Cut and sew lining

9. For the lining, select a color that is not obtrusive in a material that is not slippery. Cut the lining material using the smaller pattern. With a steam iron, mold just the top four inches around the oak tag pattern. Repeat for the other half.

10. Place the two lining pieces right side to right side and pin, cut, and sew as you did for the foundation in steps 4-8.

Interlining for foundation

11. Using the pattern for the foundation, mark and cut the interlinings for the foundation. (A 12 oz. twill or denim is recommended for interlining, but choices will vary according to the weight of the outer fabric.) The interlinings will not have seam allowances. Cut the neck angle in the interlining for the foundation.

12. With the stole laid out flat, insert the foundation interlining under the molded seam allowances. Use ¼-inch-wide Stitch Witchery® to secure the foundation interlining at the neck and along both sides of the stole, stopping several inches from the bottom. Repeat for the other half of the stole. The foundation interlining is secured with Stitch Witchery® all around. The interlining of the lining is secured at the neck area only.

Optional tassels

13. It works best to sew tassels to a piece of narrow fabric first, to get them perfectly lined up, and then sew the entire strip to the stole. To prepare optional tassels for stoles, sew placement markings onto a 1" x 6" strip of lining material. Mark the center of the tassel strip. Make two of these, one for each stole panel. Sew a tassel at each placement marking. Fold and press each strip in half at the drawn center line. Use Stitch Witchery® to hold the strip together.

Place one stole panel at a time face down on your work table. Pin the tassel strip to the bottom hem of the stole making sure that each tassel is snug up against and touching the bottom edge of the stole. Place a strip of Stitch Witchery® underneath the pinned strip and press into place. Bring the tasseled end to your sewing machine and sew in place to secure. Finally, using a herringbone stitch, hand sew the tasseled hem to the foundation interlining. Repeat this procedure for the second panel.

14. Using the pattern for the lining, draw and cut the angle of the neck in the interlinings for the lining. Butt the two ends of this interlining together and secure using a small piece of light-weight fusible interfacing. This will prevent the pieces from shifting and will provide a smooth neat base for the lining.

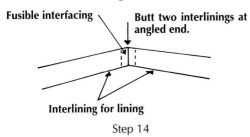

Step 14

Join interlining at neck

15. Place the foundation of the stole (now with interlinings and optional tassels in place) flat on the table right-side down. Take the interlining for the lining and place it on top of the stole so that the two interlinings are touching. Carefully line up the two pieces at the neck. You should have about ¼-inch of foundation showing on either side of the lining interlining. Carefully pin the interlining of the lining into place at the neck.

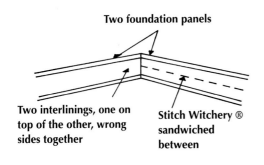

Step 15

Anchor interlining

16. Run a strip of ½-inch-wide Stitch Witchery®

down the length of the stole interlining, stopping several inches from the bottom. Fuse the two interlinings together. Repeat this procedure for the other side of the stole.

17. Trim the bottoms of the lining interlining to about ⅛-inch from the bottom of the stole.

Construction

18. Take the lining and slip the molded end over the interlining at the neck. Pin in place, aligning the neck seams of the foundation and the lining with each other.

19. Mold the lining around the interlining by hand and pin into place. At the bottom of the stoles, cut the lining material one inch longer than the stole, then tuck this end under the seam allowances of the foundation and pin into place.

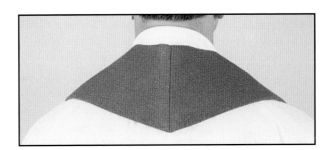

30. *Detail of Jerusalem Cross stole* by Hamel-LeSage Studio. (See plate 29.) The neck seam is sewed at an angle so that it will fit comfortably around the neck. (Photograph by Marc Hamel)

Add neck cord

20. If a neck cord is to be attached, fold the stole in half. At a point six inches down from the inside neck seam, hand sew each end of the neck cord into place. It should be far enough in so that the hand sewing will be underneath the lining and will not be seen once the lining is slip stitched into place.

21. Slip stitch the lining to the foundation.

22. Press finished stole.

2. The unlined stole

Unlined stoles are created from two pieces of fabric woven to size and joined at the back of the neck. They are hemmed at the bottom; fringes may be attached as well.

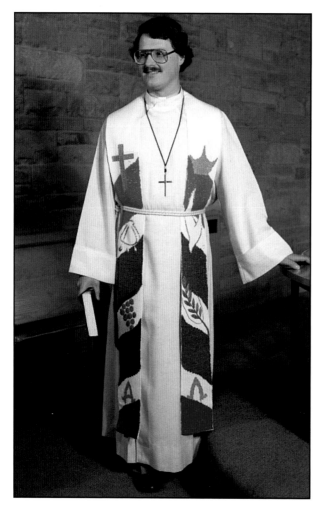

31. *Clergy stole with colors and symbols for all seasons* by Joyce Harter. Modeled by the Rev. Tom Junkert. 1984. 120" x 5½".Theo Moorman technique. Rayon and linen. Some clergy prefer to use one stole that incorporates all the colors and symbols of the church. The artist designed and wove several variations of these stoles—each had a particular meaning to the wearer because of the choice of symbols. Each was registered to its particular wearer. (Photograph by Neal Olson)

Unlined stoles work best if the fabric from which they are created is firm and somewhat stiff, since these stoles have neither lining nor interfacing. A two-ply Shetland wool sett at 24 e.p.i. will make a successful unlined stole. Consider using two threads as one for added body and color interest. As in any project, it is wise to sample if you are using yarns with which you are unfamiliar. Good selvages are very important on these stoles. Practice weaving with the yarns you have chosen, taking care to lay in, beat, change the shed, and beat again in a regular fashion until you can produce a perfect selvage.

This method of weaving a stole adapts well to techniques such as Theo Moorman, inlay, and on-loom embroidery.

1. Measure the warp in two sections and sley it with about six inches between the sections for comfortable weaving with two shuttles. Tension is important and the narrow width of each section needs to be rolled on to the warp beam with care.

2. Use two matching shuttles, one for each side of the stole. Weave a hem or plan a fringe before you begin the stole. Weave with a good, firm selvage. Use two cartoons if you are planning a design that is not loom-controlled.

3. Measure the woven fabric without tension on the warp. When the length of the stole has been woven, the back can be woven off at a 45° angle on each side, leaving enough warp ends to knot or whipstitch and join.

4. Remove the fabric from the loom and steam press on a Turkish towel on the wrong side. This pressing will give a textured surface.

5. The hems can be serged or topstitched with a satin stitch. A small strip of Stitch Witchery® fused into the hem will give added firmness and weight.

6. The 45° angle at the back of the neck can be serged or topstitched. Several finishes are possible. The ends can be interlaced with macramé knotting. A three- or four-strand braid over a seam is also a good finish.

7. A cord made of the weft yarn sewed about six inches down from the inside point across the back of the neck helps the stole lie well on most figures.

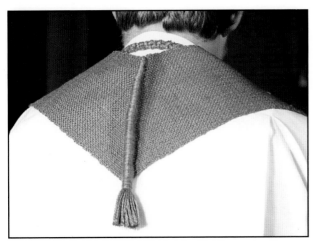

32. *Back of neck on unlined stole* by Joyce Harter. Textured Plain weave. Rayon. For a clergy stole woven in two five-inch panels, a tapered 45° angle was woven on each side after 60 inches was complete. The warp ends were knotted and worked in a macramé rib ending with a tassel. Joyce holds a 1982 copyright for this technique. An 8″ neck cord sewed to the stole six inches from the center "V" helps to hold the stole in place. (Photograph by Neal Olson)

Weave two pieces

Whatever weaving technique is used, plan to weave the stole in two side-by-side pieces. It is virtually impossible to weave a stole from one end to the other without altering the beat or the length of the design, however simple the pattern may be. Pattern elements that are supposed to be across from each other will not line up if they are not woven side-by-side.

ANOTHER UNLINED STOLE

33. *Clerical stole* by Constance Bufkin Rizner, Sevierville, Tennessee, for the Rev. Canon A. Robert Rizner. 144″ x 12″. Summer and winter. Tussah silk. Because summer and winter and the tussah provided tactile and visual textures, embellishments were limited to a cross and a simple border at the bottom of each end. The crosses and the border were embroidered in satin stitch to contrast with the more textured fabric. Threads and weave structure were chosen to create a crushed fabric, rather than a shaped neck. The unlined stole drapes well on other vestments, staying in place rather than swinging or shifting about. (Photograph by Fred Gonnerman)

3. The self-lined stole

This stole is woven in two long pieces and joined at the neck. It is constructed as a belt is constructed — with a seam down the back.

34. *Purple stole* by Lucy Brusic, St. Paul, Minnesota, for the Rev. Robert Brusic. 1993. 110" x 3¾". Crackle weave. Warp is 8/2 and 10/2 cotton; weft is 10/2 cotton and silk/wool. This stole is part of a set of crackle stoles in the colors of the church year. The pattern is an expansion of "Scandinavian Pattern" (from *Handweaver's Pattern Book* by Marguerite Davison) arranged to fit on the width of the stole. Three shades of purple were used to make the crosses more visible. (Photograph by Fred Gonnerman)

This method of constructing a stole works best if the finished stole is no more than three and one-half to four inches wide. This style is well-suited to loom-controlled patterns or all-over designs. A firm fabric such as 10/2 cotton at 22.5 e.p.i., with 5/2 for pattern weft, will not need to be interlined; lighter fabrics, such as light-weight wools, should have a three-inch strip of lightweight fusible interfacing tacked into each side.

How to make a paper pattern
A roll of adding machine paper is the right size for a cartoon for these stoles. It can be pinned to the stole as it is woven.

---

1. Wind two warps for side-by-side weaving of the two sides of the stole. It is not necessary to leave a space between the two sides of the warp because they will be woven with one shuttle, but it is helpful to have a marker thread down the center of the warp. The warp should be at least 17 inches wide to allow for shrinkage and seam allowances. The pattern motif should be centered in the middle three inches of each half of the warp, leaving at least two inches for the back on each side. It is better to have the pattern motif a little narrower than the finished stole. The parts designated for the back of the stole may be threaded to twill.

2. Weave material for a hem at the bottom of the stole and then weave the stole to its appropriate length, allowing for loom shrinkage and seam allowance. If you are quite sure of the length (or have some flexibility at the hem end) it is possible to weave a cross in crackle or some other block weave at the neck seam. Half of the motif will appear on each side of the stole; sewing the center back seam joins the two sides of the design.

3. After the stole is off the loom and the ends have been anchored, cut the fabric into two

pieces along the marker thread. Serge or overcast the cut edge. Finish the fabric as appropriate and press it. When you are ready to begin construction, clip the selvage of each piece at one-inch intervals to keep it from pulling as it hangs. If you are going to interline the stole, do so now by tacking a three-inch wide strip of lightweight interfacing down the center of the pattern.

4. Fold each piece in half right-sides together and sew along the cut/selvage seam with a ½-inch seam allowance. Stitch all the way to the bottom, but leave about six inches at the neck open on each half. Press this long seam open lightly; you do not want to create a heavy crease on the wrong side of the fabric. Stitch across the bottom of each side; clip the corners and turn the sides right side out, straightening the corners with a yardstick. Press the two parts of the stole well at this time.

5. Construct the back neck seam by putting the right sides of the seamed sides together, basting if necessary, and stitching. Press carefully and close the remaining center seam by hand. Press again.

6. A neck cord may be added to this stole as described on page 33.

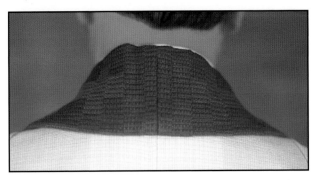

35. *Detail,* back of green stole by Lucy Brusic, St. Paul, Minnesota, for the Rev. Robert Brusic. 1990. 3" wide. Crackle weave. Warp is 10/2 cotton; weft is same and 5/2 cotton. Cross motif was divided so that it is made complete by the neck seam. A cross is frequently embroidered or affixed to the center back of a clerical stole. (Photograph by Fred Gonnerman)

THE DEACON'S STOLE

The deacon's stole can be constructed following the method for a self-lined stole. It is approximately 53 inches long from the shoulder. Two halves may be joined at the shoulder with a straight seam or the stole may be a straight 106 inches long without any seam. The two sides of the stole are connected either at the waist or at the knee by a small chain or cord. The stole is placed over the left shoulder as illustrated. If the cord is placed closer to the bottom, then the ends of the stole cross in an "X" on the right side near the knee. The deacon's stole may also have a constructed angle at the waist.

36. *Berkshire cross deacon's stole* by Pam Baker, Brimfield, Massachusetts. Available through C.M. Almy & Son, Inc., Greenwich, Connecticut. 1993. 122" x 5" tapered to 4" at shoulder. False satin in three blocks on 12 shafts. Warp is 5/2 cotton; weft is 2/8 wool. This design explored the cross symbol as an expression of wholeness. (Photograph by Tom Young for the C.M. Almy Co.)

ANOTHER NECKLINE

37 b. *Neck detail.* Six shades of blue wool were used in the warp; one color was used in the weft for fast weaving. Because of the weight of the fabric, this stole did not need an interfacing or a lining.

37 a. *Baptismal stole* by Linda Hicks Hall, Gahanna, Ohio, for the Rev. Todd E. Frail. 1993. 105" x 5". Twill. Warp and weft are wool. This stole was commissioned by the Stonybrook United Methodist Church as a parting gift for their pastor. Two sacraments are observed in the Methodist church: baptism and communion. The dove and the shell which have been appliquéed on this stole are symbols of baptism. The appliquéed forms are made of Ultrasuede® and padded with felt.

37 c. *Inside neck detail.* After careful fitting on the wearer, the center back was cut with a rotary cutter and the edges serged. The center seam was then sewed by hand on a 45° angle and the ends were stitched down. This finish provides weight so that the stole does not slide when it is worn over a robe. (Photograph by Fred Gonnerman)

A SHAPED HEM

AN UNUSUAL CROSS

38. *Stole* by Helen Sandvig, Lynwood, Washington, for Cedar Cross United Methodist Church, Mill Creek, Washington. 1992. 188" x 6". Undulating twill. 18/2 wool. This stole in greens has a pattern suggesting palm leaves. It is part of a parament set of five pieces with colors to blend with the forest setting that is in view above and beside the altar. It was necessary to enlarge the pattern so that it would show at a distance. (Photograph by Thomas Sandvig)

39. *Festal stole* by Bryan Paatz, Portland, Oregon. Private collection. 1993. 112" x 5". Twill variation. Rayon warp with weft of wool, cotton, and Lurex. The inspiration for this stole was the diaper patterns in the backgrounds of twelfth and thirteenth century manuscript paintings. The metallic gallooning that separates the red bands was created by depressing a single treadle for the distance of the band. The white portion of the stole is a series of random treadlings which serve as a textured foil for the decorative bandings. The tabby in this section is a very fine Lurex. Negative space, created by couched metallic and wool yarns, implies a cross form. (Photograph by the artist)

40. *Advent chasuble, stole, and burse* by Joyce Rettstadt. 1981. Monk's belt. All natural fibers in the weft. This Advent chasuble is made from commercial raw silk with a handwoven orphrey. The design represents an inexpensive line of vesture offered as an alternative to custom-designed, handwoven sets. The orphrey is a non-repeating sequence of 20 monochromatic colors. (Photograph by Nash Studio)

The beauty of future vesture should be determined by the quality of its fabric, its cut and workmanship, and by the simplicity and dignity of its design.

Katreen Bettencourt, "Tradition Not Trends"
Modern Liturgy 19, no. 1(February 1992)

Chapter 4
VESTMENTS
by Joyce Rettstadt

41. *St. Gregory chasuble* by Hamel-LeSage Studio for Immaculate Conception Church, Malden, Massachusetts. 1994. 51" long x 72" wide. Twill. Warp and weft are wool/silk. This piece was woven in a 3/1 twill on a fuschia warp with a deep purple weft so that it gives the appearance of being lined. The attached orphrey panel is a summer and winter polychrome design inspired by an icon of St. Gregory of Nyssa. (Photograph by Marc Hamel)

O UR SENSES are aroused by smell, touch, taste, sight, and sound. Fine cooks know that a meal can be thought of as a ritual that engages our senses through symbolic and non-verbal elements. Think of the meals in movies such as *Babette's Feast* (1987) or *Like Water for Chocolate (1992)*. The ritual of a festive meal includes invitations, variety, pattern, and plot — in addition to the food. The Eucharist is just such a festive meal, where all the aesthetic details matter. Vestments are "dressing for the meal" — ritual clothing for ritual activity.

Vestments have names and features that denote their importance for the ritual in which they are used. The alb is the basic garment worn by clergy; it is usually, but not always, bound with a cincture. Ordained clergy wear the stole about the neck and hanging over both shoulders; the deacon wears the stole crossed over the left shoulder and fastened low on the right side of the body. (See chapter 3 for a discussion of the liturgical stole.) The chasuble, when used, is worn at the Eucharist by the presiding minister. The dalmatic is a sleeved garment worn over the alb and the deacon's stole; it is the vestment proper to deacons. The cope is worn by liturgical leaders in procession and in festival services.

Vestments as a link to the past

In addition to being part of the aesthetic appeal of the Eucharistic celebration in liturgical churches, vestments for Christian worship link us to the earliest centuries of the church. The form of Christian liturgical garments comes from the ordinary dress of the Graeco-Roman world. It was not until the fifth or sixth century that the clothing worn by those officiating at the liturgy began to differ from that worn by the general population. The change came, according to one historian, when barbarians swept down from northern Europe and introduced trousers to Rome. The clergy kept sartorial faith by continuing to wear the everyday garb of imperial Rome.

Over the centuries, many reforming and revitalizing impulses have influenced the look and shape of today's vestments. For example, during the Reformation, some Protestant leaders eliminated traditional vestments (as well as other textiles, sculpture, paintings, and visual art) and wore the Geneva gown—the academic dress of the period. At the beginning of the twentieth century, vestments as we now know them were used infrequently. Some clergy wore academic gowns; other, such as Lutherans, wore a cassock and surplice.

Recent liturgical renewal has tended to re-emphasize the arts in worship. In France, during the early part of the twentieth century, Father Marie-Alain Couturier joined the Ateliers d'Art Sacré, a workshop devoted to renewing liturgical art. Couturier's vision was to commission the greatest artists of his time to express the transcendent. At about the same time in the United States, Maurice Lavanoux became the editor of *Liturgical Arts*, a Benedictine magazine which sought to bring liturgical information to artists, architects, and those who were leading liturgy.

Then, in the late 1940s, Sister Augustina Flüeler started an atelier in Stans, Switzerland, where she revived the use of the ancient conical form of the chasuble, and designed a *tunica* which was to take the place of the alb and chasuble. Flüeler was the first designer to use historical research to recover the forms of ancient vestments. In addition, by handweaving the fabric from which the vestments were made, Flüeler found she could control the whole process from concept to reality.

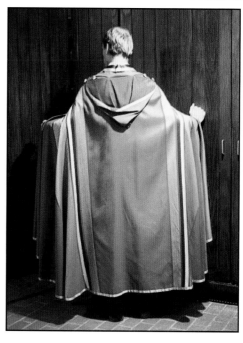

42. *Green cope* from Sister Augustina Flüeler's workshop. Owned by the Abbey of Saint John, Collegeville, Minnesota. (Photograph by Charles Pohlmann)

At about the same time, the Benedictine Abbaye of St. André in Bruges, Belgium, published a periodical, *L'art d'église*. A supplement, *L'ouvroir liturgique*, displayed handwoven fabrics and patterns for making fuller vestments, including the conical chasuble.

In 1963, Vatican II provided a motive force for changes in all liturgical life. The altar was moved out from the rear of the chancel and the presiding priest was instructed to stand behind the altar facing the worshipers. The General Instruction on the Roman Missal (1973) stated that "the beauty of a vestment should derive from its material and form rather than its ornamentation." In 1978, a document by the Bishops' Committee on the Liturgy, Environment, and Art in Catholic Worship, further defined the role of liturgical clothing:

1. Ritual vestment for ministers is an appropriate symbol of their service.
2. It is a "helpful aesthetic component of the rite."

The document went on to state, "The more these vestments fulfill their function by their color, design, and enveloping form, the less they will need the signs, slogans, and symbols which an unkind history has fastened on them."

Today, because of this liturgical renewal, vestments are more widely used in Episcopal and Lutheran churches. Several other Protestant churches have begun suggesting the alb and stole for ordained ministers.

General considerations

A vestment is a symbol in and of itself; it does not need words or symbols. Aidan Kavanaugh says that the "vestment is not costume. The sacredness [of the vestment] derives from the nature of the events in which [the vestment] is worn."*

Vesture should not focus on the presider but on the whole Eucharistic setting and the congregation for which it was designed. Nonetheless, vestments are clothing and must take account of the bodies that inhabit them. They should be full, enveloping, and draping—not stiff or "board-like." Use rich, bold colors that can be seen at a distance. The color and design of the vestments help to focus and lead the eye to the ritual action.

Robert Hovda's advice to worship committees and donors is to "search out an artist who is attuned to the liturgy to create the object..."** As an artist, you can enhance your confidence with donors and church committees and increase your chances for success by knowing the traditions of the group with which you are working, attending a worship service, and experiencing the space and the liturgy.

---

* Aidan Kavanaugh, "Liturgical Vesture in the Roman Catholic Tradition" *Raiment for the Lord's Service* (Chicago: Art Institute of Chicago: 1975) 14.

**Robert Hovda, "The Vesting of Liturgical Ministers" (*Worship,* March 1980) 100.

Handweaving basics for liturgical garments

Use the finest natural materials available to you. Suitable fibers for vestments are lightweight wools, wool/silks, pure silks, and even cotton if it is of excellent quality. The "hand" or drape of the fabric is very important. Fabric that wrinkles easily should not be used.

43. *Vestment for Pentecost and Reformation* by Marjorie Ford for the Rev. Paul Lindstrom. 1983. 50" long x 54" wide. Warp-faced plain weave with supplementary weft. Warp is 20/2 cotton, weft is 2/8 wool; supplementary weft is wool. Since the owner of this vestment would be using it in a variety of spaces, the physical environment was less important than a focus on the role of the wearer. The graphic design is larger in scale on the back—the area that is visible when the celebrant is processing. It is more intimate in scale on the front—the area seen as the celebrant faces the congregation when the Eucharist is distributed. The symbolism is based on John 3:8 "The wind blows where it will; you hear the sound of it but you do not know where it comes from, or where it is going. So with everyone who is born from the Spirit." The flow of curved shapes on the back of the garment suggests this flowing action of the Spirit. (Photograph by the artist)

Any weave structure is acceptable as long as it follows the above guidelines. A summer and winter weave, which is often used for upholstery, may work for a vestment using a 60/2 silk in the warp and a 12/2 silk pattern thread with a 60/2 silk tabby. A twill-derived weave drapes better than a plain weave. Needless to say, you should always weave a sample and finish it before undertaking a large project.

Remember that vestments are usually viewed at a distance even though weavers make design and color choices with their eyes about 25 inches from the weaving surface. Viewing your samples at a distance will help you to make intelligent decisions.

Inlay work may be placed where needed, using a Moorman inlay technique or other weave structure such as a crepe or twill as long as the areas of inlay are not too large. Supplementary warp and/or weft is another way to place color where you want it. Make sure, however, that the floats are not so long that they catch on objects.

The easiest way to design a warp is to work on graph paper with properly scaled pattern pieces cut from a contrasting paper. That way, areas of color or pattern may be accurately planned. Do not forget to allow for loom waste and at least 15% shrinkage. A coordinated set of vestments may be woven on a long warp with accurate planning and creative use of color in the warp. This may mean that the color in the warp is not symmetrical.

Handwoven fabrics should be handwashed. Soap is not necessary unless the yarns contain machine oils.

Above all, take care in the construction. Just as the finest materials should be chosen for the weaving of the cloth, so great care should be taken with finishing. If you are not skilled at sewing, consider hiring a tailor or seamstress to work with you.

THE ALB

Even though an alb is rarely handwoven, a discussion of vestments should begin with this garment. Derived from the tunic, the alb is the first garment to be put on over street clothes when vesting. It is usually belted with a rope cincture. Cinctures are almost always white or neutral. They may be custom-made with a rope machine.

The alb

The alb is also the first liturgical garment to be mentioned in church history. In a text found in the Apostolic Tradition of Hippolytus in the early third century, newly initiated and baptized members were presented with white robes to signify their new life in Christ.

By the twelfth century the records clearly defined the alb as a liturgical vestment and spelled out that it was to be made of linen, with specific characteristics. It was to have tight sleeves, and a long full skirt. If it was decorated, it was to have four or five "apparels"—decorative panels—one on each sleeve, one each on the center of the front and the back skirt near the bottom. If a fifth "apparel" was used, it was near the neck opening. Apparels are shown in plate 2 on page 3.

In the alb, handweavers have an opportunity for the creation of a full enveloping garment that would be attractive to Reformed pastors who wear only the alb and the stole.

Traditional techniques using linen or lovely cottons, with areas of leno lace or applied "apparels" may be especially useful. Basic commercial patterns could be adapted and modified to suit your needs. You may want to consult commercial supply houses to study variations in style.

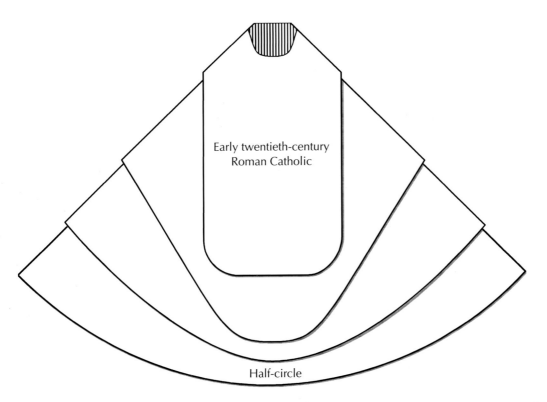

Early twentieth-century
Roman Catholic

Half-circle

Progressive reductions in the size of the chasuble reduced it from a semi-circle to a short garment resembling a sandwich board. *Drawing by William D. McTeer after Augustina Flüeler.*

THE CHASUBLE—HISTORY AND FORM

The chasuble may be worn by the presider at the Eucharist. The word "chasuble" is derived from Latin *casula* meaning "little house." This garment originated from a cloak made from a semi-circle of wool or animal hides called a *paenula*, which was opened in the front and buttoned at the neck. Originally, the chasuble reached down to the feet so that the arms could not be used except by doubling the border of the vestment up and over the wrists, or throwing it onto the shoulder.

The chasuble has taken many forms over time, varying by period and country. It has changed in use as well. In the eighth century, according to *Ordo Romanus Primus*, all ranks of the clergy entered the sanctuary wearing the chasuble. However, only the celebrant retained his while the others removed theirs and handed them to the acolytes. Over subsequent cen-

turies, the most common change (as in all of the vestments) was an abbreviation. The practice of elevating of the Host in the fourteenth century required that the arms of the priest be free to move, hence the chasuble was folded back onto the priest's shoulders by the deacon.

This liturgical action, which coincided with the addition of elaborate jeweled decoration, the invention of heavy cut velvets, and the fashion of *Opus Anglicanum* embroidery, began to alter the shape of the chasuble. It changed from a half-circle that was seamed to form a conical shape with a crosswise drape in the front to a much narrower shape that came to the elbow and had shoulder seams. Eventually, it was cut even shorter at the sides to look like a sandwich-board with two stiff pieces of fabric attached at the shoulders.

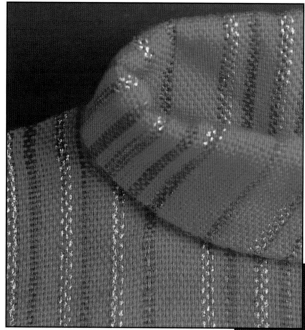

GOTHIC CHASUBLE

44 a. *Red chasuble.* 44 b. *Detail of cowl collar.*
Suzanne Halvorson, Bloomington, Indiana, for Saints
Peter and Paul Cathedral, Indianapolis, Indiana. Sewed
by Evelyn Forthofer, OSF. 1995. 57" long x 57" wide.
Plain weave. Cotton, rayon, silk, metallic. The fabric of
this brilliant red chasuble is both lightweight and
graceful. A small amount of green is used in the fabric
to make it shimmer and give the color depth. The cowl
collar design was created by the Carmelite Sisters of
Terre Haute, Indiana, and adapted for use with
handwoven fabric. (Photographs by Tyagan Miller)

The Eastern equivalent of the chasuble is the *phelonion*. It is similar to the conical chasuble except that it is cut very short just across the chest (to about elbow-height) resulting in a bell-shaped garment that is very comfortable to wear. It frees the arms and is attractive in form, since the long back area fills with air when the priest is walking.

Several forms of chasubles may be constructed by modern weavers. Though they are all based on variations of historic shapes, modern methods may be used in the production and construction.

Gothic and contemporary chasubles

The term Gothic is a misnomer, as this chasuble shape has little or no connection with the Gothic period. It is a name given to a shape by commercial vestment makers. The contemporary chasuble is a basic clothing shape. These shapes have a sloped shoulder seam that drops four or more inches from the neck to the wrist area. As the angle of the shoulder line drops, the garment tends to form the same bell shape as the conical chasuble.

Patterns for Gothic and contemporary chasubles may be found on pages 140 and 141. Both patterns are scaled for a person who is about 5'10" tall.

If your loom is wide enough, you may turn the pattern and cut the Gothic style or the contemporary style with the warp running across the garment. If you have a narrow loom, weave two long pieces of fabric the desired length and seam them at the center, covering the seam with an orphrey if desired. Or you may divide the pattern into four quarters with the warp running vertically. You may also weave the material as a single fabric twice the warp width.

It is a good idea to make a muslin version of your pattern pieces before starting a large project. You will understand the construction process and be able to identify problem areas before you begin. In addition, you can decide the exact placement of stripes and design elements by drawing them on the muslin.

Calculating the fabric needed

The recommended length of a chasuble is from 51" to 55" depending upon the height of the wearer. The hem should come below the calf of the leg. The width of the chasuble should be at least 62" from wrist to wrist, preferably more. (Remember that a man's shirt sleeve length is determined by the measurement from the center back to the wrist, so the average 33-inch sleeve would require a chasuble width of at least 66 inches.) Ideally, the garment should be full enough that some of the fabric is gathered up on the wrist to create a more graceful line.

Construction

Seam the shoulders. Make a front seam, if there is to be one, and cover it with an orphrey if you wish. These garments should be completely finished inside as well as outside. Consider using French seams or flat-felled seams where orphreys will not be used. Orphreys may be interlined to create body, especially if they are wide. Then hem the garment. The hem is "molded" as described on page 31 and ironed in.

The neck may be finished with a double thickness of bias material to make a rolled edge, or it may have a facing. A rolled collar may also be used. These neck treatments are the same as those used in regular garment construction. Double stitch the neck seam as the neck takes much abuse. You may also cut a narrow selvage edge from lining materials and stitch it into the back neck seam to prevent stretching. No matter what the shape of the neck is, a neck opening of approximately 27 inches in circumference is suggested, so that the wearer's head can pass through easily.

CONICAL CHASUBLE

45. *Conical chasuble with stole, burse, and veil* by Joyce Rettstadt. 1991. Twill variation. Pure silk. This was a special commission to produce an ancient style of chasuble. Warp and weft yarns were the same except for the orphrey material which was woven with a 20/2 burgundy mercerized cotton (doubled) and fine Lurex as a tabby between pattern shots, thus enlarging the design. A detail of the orphrey appears on page 23. (Photograph by Nash Studio)

The conical chasuble

The circle and the ellipse were ancient symbols of spiritual perfection. Although this encircling form creates a beautiful garment, it is difficult to wear unless the presider is properly trained. This form is unlined and requires a fabric that drapes well.

A pattern for a conical chasuble can be found on page 142. The pattern is for a figure that is approximately 5'10". Adjust the pattern as needed for your particular commission. The remarks that follow refer to this pattern.

Making a pattern

Make a rectangle of oak tag pattern paper 120" long and 60" wide. Fold to make two 60-inch squares. Draw a diagonal (as shown) and find the point 25½ inches on the line beyond the corner of the square where the diagonal touches the fold. This point will be the center of the radius for the half-circle shape. Draw the shape and cut a pattern which represents the finished size of the garment.

To design the neck opening, make a pencil mark 3¼ inches down the center and 11⅜ inches in each direction from the center. At this outer point, draw a perpendicular line 1⅝ inches long to the diameter line of the half circle. Now connect the bottom of this line to the first mark at the center. (See pattern on page 142.).

Calculating the fabric needed

Handwoven fabric finished at about 42 inches wide is perfect for this shape. Three pieces, each slightly longer than 62 inches, are pieced along the selvage edges. Orphrey bands may be used to cover the seams. Cut a separate piece of fabric to face the neck area.

Construction

With the wrong side of the fabric facing up, place the oak tag on the joined fabric one inch from the straight edge. Weight the pattern securely and mark one inch from the edge of the curved edge. Cut carefully.

Do not remove the pattern. Use a steam iron to "mold" fabric over the pattern for the hem. Turn the raw edge under with your fingers and press again. (This "molding" is the same technique used in the Hamel-LeSage Studio instructions for stole-making. See page 31.) Hem by hand or machine.

Fold edges together to form a conical shape and seam to the neck area. Cover this seam with an orphrey. Finish neck area with facing.

I do not suggest a lining for a chasuble. It is difficult to find two fabrics that are compatible. The lining will look fine for a while, but after several cleanings it will be found hanging in unattractive positions at the hemline. A lining also increases the weight of the garment.

Five ways to weave a chasuble

The fabric for a chasuble may be handwoven in one of five ways:

1. If your loom is wide enough, you can weave the chasuble in two pieces and cut it crossways of the loom; that is, with the warp running crossways.

2. You may cut the chasuble in two long, narrow pieces, with a center seam both front and back. The chasuble will be an elongated, but symmetrical ellipse.

3. You may cut the fabric in four pieces with both shoulder and center seams. The back section should be from two to three inches longer than the front.

4. You may cut the chasuble in one piece, as a large elongated ellipse with no seams.

5. You may weave the fabric in three strips—a center section and a right and a left section.

CONTEMPORARY CHASUBLE

46 a. *White chasuble with matching stole* by Joyce Harter for First English Lutheran Church, Cannon Falls, Minnesota. 1987. Plain weave to produce a double width fabric. Rayon and linen. This chasuble was made on a five-yard warp with gold warps running the length of it. The fabric was finished with a professional steam pressing; two curved sections were cut for the front and the back and sewed at a slight angle for the shoulders. Bias strips from the leftover corners were interfaced to form a stand-up collar. A hem-stitched hem was worked around the entire garment and the collar so that the only raw edges were at the shoulder seams.

46 b. (below) *Detail* of cross form on the front of the chasuble. Log cabin technique. (Photographs by Fred Gonnerman)

DALMATIC

47. *Red dalmatic* by Joyce Rettstadt. Private collection. 1996. Plain weave and twill. 2/18 silk/wool. This dalmatic was constructed from a special pattern using an inverted pleat at the shoulders. The design was influenced by the experimental work done of Sr. Flüeler in creating timeless designs for vestments. The bands of color suggest the ancient *clavi* (bands). (Photograph by Hamel-LeSage Studio)

The dalmatic was introduced into Roman society from Dalmatia in the late second century. An ample garment with wide sleeves, the dalmatic, like the alb, was derived from the tunic.

Although the Romans disdained the dalmatic because of its barbarian origins, it slowly gained in favor until, in the fourth century, the emperor Constantine wore it as a mark of mag-

isterial dignity. Constantine also permitted the Christian Bishop of Rome to wear the dalmatic as a sign of his new authority within the state.

Eventually, however, the dalmatic came to be preferred for the diaconal role in the liturgy; the deacon could move his arms more freely with sleeves than he could in the conical chasuble.

The dalmatic was frequently decorated with bands of purple cloth *(clavi)*, running over the shoulders from front to back and on the edge of the sleeves.

Over the centuries, the dalmatic, like the chasuble, was shortened from ankle-length to knee-length or shorter. The weight and stiffness of the elaborate embroideries applied to it meant that it was no longer seamed under the arms. For a period of time, dalmatics were fastened by ties under the arms and at the sides above the waist. (Interestingly, this form, when spread out flat, has the shape of a Greek cross.) Elaborate cords and tassels were often added at the edge of the neck area; two decorative apparels, one at the chest and the other at knee level, (both front and back) were also added.

Today, in the West, the deacon wears the dalmatic on festive occasions. In many Eastern churches, the *sakkos*, an older form of the dalmatic, is worn as the outer garment both by bishops and deacons.

Construction of a dalmatic

The pattern shown on page 143 works best if it is cut in three long pattern pieces (placing the patterns on a fold as shown). This construction eliminates a seam along the top of the sleeves and is an authentic reproduction of the ancient garment. Finish the seams and "mold" the hems. (See page 31). Cover the seams with bands. The neck may be edged with a banding to eliminate stretching.

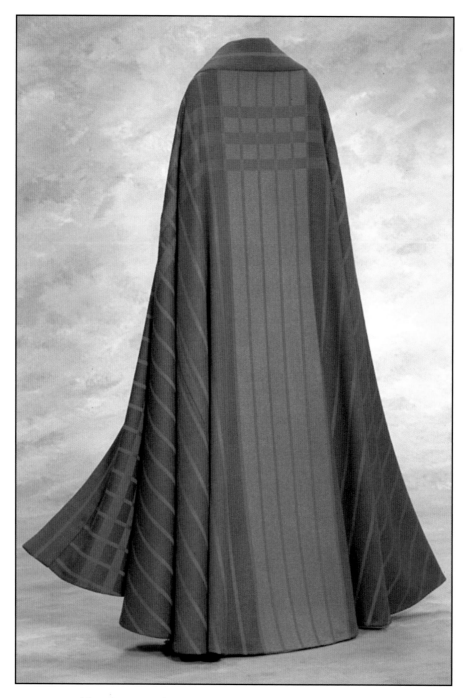

48. *Reversible Advent cope* by Joyce Rettstadt, for the Rev. Andrew Ciferni, O. Praem. 1994. 58" from the base of neck to hem. Twill. 2/18 silk/wool. The reversed twill creates a reversible fabric. The garment is constructed so that it may be worn with either side showing. Tailored from pattern on page 144 of this book. (Photograph by Nash Studio)

Cope

The cope appeared in the eighth century as a processional garment worn both by clergy and nobility. The basic shape is like the *paenula*—a full half-circle. The cope is a long cloak—open down the front with some type of closure at the neck area. Since the ancient cope was an outer garment, it usually had a hood to cover the head. The shield-like shape frequently seen on the back of a cope is a vestigial form of that hood. Today it is just an area for ornamentation and is not a necessary part of the construction.

The closure of the cope may be a permanent wide band of fabric or a two-piece clasp (morse) that can be made of various materials such as gold, silver, or cast bronze.

The cope is used primarily for ceremony. Usually in the appropriate liturgical color, it is worn over the alb (or surplice) for processions and festival services other than the Eucharist. It may be worn by the principle leaders of the service, whether ordained or not. The bishop may wear it for baptisms or marriages or when assisting at gatherings and councils.

Construction of a cope

The pattern given on page 144 is a full half-circle with the radius for the pattern being the desired finished length from the base of the neck to the hem. The cope is left open in the front; an orphrey is attached to the straight edges. (Figure the width of the orphrey into the radius used to construct the pattern.) The orphrey should be interlined and lined. A decision must also be made about the fastening technique. If a permanent morse is attached, make sure that it is reinforced at the point of joining the main body of the cope as it will take much strain during use.

The fabric for a cope may be pieced several ways. If a complicated woven pattern is used, the cope may be designed with pie-shaped pieces that retain the integrity and direction of the pattern. A cope may also be pieced as suggested for the conical chasuble (three pieces sewed along the selvages—see page 49).

The weight of the fabric woven for a cope may be slightly heavier than fabric used for a chasuble. It should drape well but have a bit more body. Interior finishing is especially important since the inside is sometimes seen when the wearer is walking in procession. A woven 3/1 twill is especially nice for a cope; the different color on the reverse side adds interest.

Care of Handwoven Vestments

When you complete a stole or a set of vestments and paraments, write up instructions for the care and storage of these items. These instructions will help whoever is responsible for caring for your carefully created vestments. An example is provided below.

Caretaking

- This handwoven item has some wool weft. If moths are a problem in your area, take this into consideration when storing the item.
- Prolonged exposure to direct sunlight is detrimental to any fiber.
- Store this item flat, if possible, with padding at all folds.
- When taking the item out of storage, steam by holding steam iron above the wrinkled area. If this does not remove creases and wrinkles, then press lightly with a pressing cloth on the right side of the item. Use a steam iron and an up and down motion rather than a sliding motion.
- Extreme heat is also harmful to this fabric. Check your iron before using. Most wrinkles will easily come out of this fabric just by hanging it for a few days before use.
- When cleaning, use a reputable dry cleaning establishment and make sure the workers realize that the item is handwoven. Ask that it be hand-dry-cleaned instead of vat-cleaned.
- With proper care, this item should serve you well for many years.

THE MORSE

The morse is a two-part fastening device used on copes. It is the only device used to hold a cope on the wearer and is often the occasion for elaboration and decoration. The word *morse* is synonymous with *fibula*.

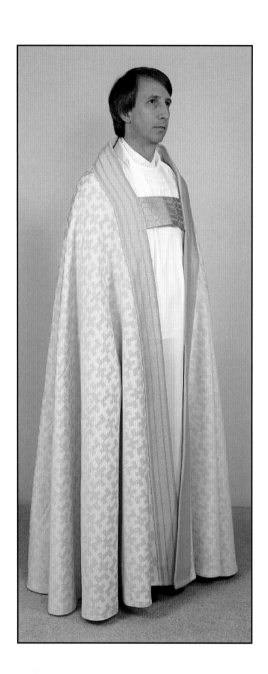

49 a. (left) *Gold cope* by Hamel-LeSage Studio for the Rev. Andrew Ciferni. 1994. 60" semicircle. Summer and winter. Wool/silk/cotton/gold. This cope was woven in a cross pattern inspired by the brickwork on the façade of the cathedral in Aquila, Italy. The foundation is a white wool/silk warp and a hand dyed gold silk weft. The gold orphrey is woven in twill, with the same hand dyed silk for weft, on a 10/2 cotton warp.

49 b. (above) *Morse for gold cope* by Edward LeSage of Hamel LeSage Studio. 1994. 4" x 8". Twill. Cotton and gold. This morse was woven on a gold cotton warp with a fine gold metallic weft, which packed to about 120 picks per inch. This morse is fastened permanently on both sides; the cope, an old Anglican style, must be put on over the wearer's head. (Photographs by Marc Hamel)

The Mitre

The mitre is a bishop's hat. It may be worn during processions, baptisms, and blessings. It is removed during the Eucharist. Several people who make mitres say they figured out how to make them by taking mitres apart, but directions may be found in *Church Needlework* by Beryl Dean.

51. *Mitre pretiosa with lappets* by Bryan Paatz, Portland, Oregon. Private collection. 1994. 10" high by 12½ inches wide. Lappets are 23 inches long including fringe. Twill-overshot variation. Warp and weft are rayon Lurex. A utilitarian twill has been adapted for ecclesiastical use by using metallic threads. Couched Japanese gold thread and stones were added to enhance the opulence of the fabric. A round Lurex thread was used; round threads give visual depth and luster. However, since overshot repetitions tend to be unstable, a very fine flat Lurex was used for the tabby passes between the overshots. (Photograph by the artist)

50. *Bishop's mitre* by Marc Hamel of Hamel-LeSage Studio. Private collection. 1993. 9" high x 12" wide. Plaited twill. Warp is 2/18 wool/silk. Both the white foundation and the gold orphrey were woven on the same wool/silk warp. The foundation weft is also wool/silk. The orphrey is a twill stripe woven with gold metallic weft at 120 picks per inch. The stripe design was inspired by a chasuble woven by Augustina Flüeler. (Photograph by Marc Hamel)

52 a. (detail) *Pentecost paraments* by Åsa Blake, Atlanta, Georgia, for North Decatur Presbyterian Church, Decatur, Georgia. 1987. Theo Moorman technique. 10/2 perle cotton for the ground; 20/2 perle cotton for the tie-down. Weft is 8/2 cotton, 20/2 (doubled or tripled) and novelty yarns. The artist was asked to use flames—the symbol for Pentecost—on the seasonal green background. The green had to be similar to the color of the carpet in the sanctuary. In addition to red for the flames, she chose varying shades of purple and yellow.

52 b. (upper left) *Communion table parament.* 78" x 30". The outer flames curve to the center to conform to the triangular shape of the sanctuary. The parament was lined by hand with purchased cotton fabric.

52 c. (lower right) *Pulpit parament.* 22" x 30". A separate length of plain green fabric was woven and sewed to the top of the design panel to support the panel and cover the table top. The pulpit and altar hangings were designed to work either as a unit or individually.(Photographs by Bruce Parsons)

Chapter 5
PARAMENTS
by Joyce Harter

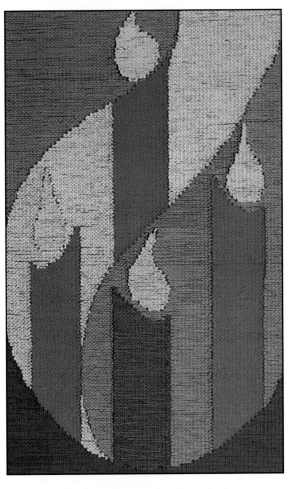

53. *Detail of pulpit parament for Advent* by Joyce Harter for Eventide Lutheran Home, Moorhead, Minnesota. 1992. 32" x 18". Theo Moorman technique. Wool, rayon, cotton. Candles symbolize the light coming into the world at the season of Advent, the four weeks before Christmas. Color blending in the Moorman technique made it possible to realize the design in various shades of blue. The design was inspired by a church bulletin cover. (Photograph by Eventide Lutheran Home)

PARAMENTS ARE the hangings that dress the altar and chancel furniture. Paraments serve to draw the attention of worshipers to the altar and the pulpit; in most churches that follow the liturgical year, the paraments change with the colors of the church year and so give a sense of movement and drama. Many liturgical churches have five sets of paraments—blue for Advent, white for Christmas and Easter, purple for Lent, green for the season of Epiphany and the long season of Pentecost, and red for festivals. (A more detailed discussion of the use of color in Protestant and Roman Catholic churches is found on page 15.)

Because the shapes of altars and pulpits are unique and the colors site-specific, craftspersons are often asked to design individualized paraments. Although the temptation is to show off one's skill as a weaver, it is important to remember that the function of a parament is to add beauty and dignity to a place of worship. As with clergy stoles, these articles should enhance the worship experience rather than trying to stand alone as a work of art. The fine distinction of a parament that affirms the place and rightness of handcrafted work in a sanctuary without drawing attention to itself is difficult to achieve, but it is an ideal worth seeking.

Every item of cloth used in the church has a name and a specified use. These items are usually organized according to the piece of furniture they cover.

Altar and table coverings

The altar or table where the Eucharistic elements are consecrated serves as one of the centers of worship. (The other center is the pulpit.) Altars are usually, but not always, raised slightly above the floor level on which the congregation stands. They may be made of stone, wood, or metal. They may be rectangular, square, or even oval.

At one time, altars were firmly attached to the wall of the church. Under the influence of the liturgical movement of the last three decades, it has become common for altars to be freestanding. Some are placed in the middle of a circular church. Because of the importance of the altar for worship and its relative distance from the congregation, the scale of the parament is crucial to its success.

Two extremes are to be avoided. One is covering the altar so completely that the viewer has no idea of what is holding it up. The other is putting small hangings or small designs on a large altar. Experiment with a piece of fabric or paper to determine the correct proportions. It is also helpful to look carefully at other paraments that have been successful (or not) on a specific altar.

For altars that are against the wall or, because of architectural necessity, attached to the wall, the following shapes are possible.

- A *full frontal* hangs nearly to the floor, covering the full front of the altar.

- A *superfrontal* hangs 12 to 14 inches down from the top of the altar, but runs the full length (or nearly the full length) of the altar.

- An *antependium* (sometimes called an *altar cover*) is a single piece of fabric, definitely shorter than the full length of the altar, that hangs in the center of the altar.

- *Two or more hangings* can be used on a long altar, or on either side of a carving or other centrally placed decoration.

54. *Pair of hangings for Pentecost season* by Ann Williamsen, Lyons, Colorado, for First Lutheran Church, Longmont, Colorado. 1994. Each is 28″ x 8″. Single pick-up double weave. Cottolin. This weaving for a small moveable altar was designed to complement the informal setting in which it would be used. During the summer, services take place in an outdoor courtyard, with colorful flowers. The artist designed a pattern of multi-colored crosses on a green background to express the exuberant life and growth of the garden and the season. (Photograph by the artist)

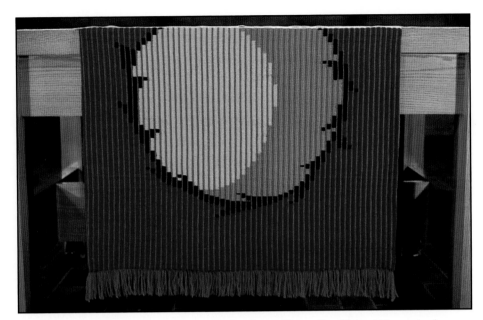

55. *"A Lenten Embrace,"* altar parament by Elaine Olson, Eau Claire, Wisconsin, for Luther Seminary, St. Paul, Minnesota. 1986. 42" x 30" including fringe. Overshot. Wool. The challenge in this setting was to create a parament that would complement the monumental simplicity of the worship space while focusing attention on the altar. The crown of thorns is a Lenten motif. This antependium is interlined with fusible rayon and lined with commercial polyester/cotton. A detail of this piece appears on page 22. (Photograph by Fred Gonnerman)

56. *Full altar frontal* by Barbara Berg, Decorah, Iowa, for Shepherd of the Hills Lutheran Church, Edina, Minnesota. 1993. 10' x 3'. Theo Moorman technique. Wool, rayon, cotton. This parament was intended for Advent, but consultation between the artist and the committee resulted in less blue and more gold and white than the original design. As a result the parament set (it includes pulpit and lectern falls) is used for Advent, Christmas, and Epiphany. The light rays on this altar frontal are intended to imply the shape of a creche. (Photograph by Kim Skistad)

57. *Laudian altar cover* by Edna Gonske *(dec.)* for Luther Seminary, St. Paul, Minnesota. 1986. 140" x 118". Summer and winter. Wool. Red is the color for Pentecost, martyrs, saints' days, Reformation, and certain festivals. The setting is completed by a simple pulpit hanging. (Photograph by Fred Gonnerman)

58. *Lenten altar hangings* by Joyce Harter for Grace Lutheran Church, Schenectady, New York. 1986. 25" wide x 33" long. Theo Moorman technique. Wool, rayon, and cotton. The bold crown of thorns with dark striations reminds Christians of the sufferings of Christ. The design was created to be understood at a distance and close up. Because the Theo Moorman technique was used, the paraments did not need to be lined, although the hem is reinforced with fusible tape to keep it straight. These paraments go over the table and hang down the back. (Photograph by Fred Gonnerman)

59. *Hangings for a square altar* by Joyce Harter for Bethel Lutheran Church, Northfield, Minnesota. 1989. Four runners, each 130" x 12".Theo Moorman technique. Wool and rayon. The 48"-square wood altar needed hangings that would enclose but not overshadow it. The dove and the flames are symbols of the Holy Spirit. The runners, which are a firm fabric and unlined, can be positioned in several ways. (Photograph by Fred Gonnerman)

Communion tables

For altars or communion tables that stand away from the wall, the following shapes are possible.

- *A laudian hanging* is a full cover for the altar; it hangs to the floor and covers the table front and back.

- *Centered or dual hangings* can be fastened on the front and back of the altar, or they can go over the top of the altar.

- *A shaped hanging* can be placed off center.

- *Lengthwise runners* are appropriate for an altar that is viewed from all sides.

- *A square altar* can have equal length runners that cross over each other.

Sometimes these tables are viewed from all sides, so it necessary to have a four--way design.

All of these hangings can be woven in seasonal colors. Different styles can be used in different seasons within the same chancel setting.

It is not always necessary to weave a piece long enough to cover the top of the communion table as the table will frequently be covered with a fair linen. However, if you do not weave a piece long enough to cross the communion table, you will have to devise some method to hold the front and the back panels together, such as a muslin or linen top.

OTHER ALTAR WEAVINGS

Fair linens

Many churches protect the altar and the paraments from the stains caused by communion wine and candle wax by covering the top of the altar with a washable, white fair linen. This cloth may be of pure linen or of some wash-and-wear fabric. The fair linen can be the same size as the top of the altar or it can hang some distance down the sides. The fair linen may have five crosses worked into it, one in each corner and one in the center.

60 b. *Detail* of wrapped-warp cross. This equilateral cross (also called a Greek cross) measures three inches by three inches. (Photograph by the artist)

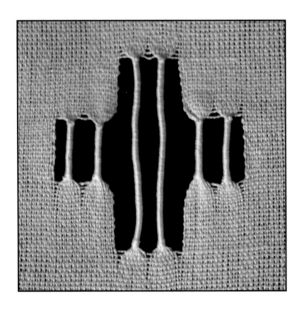

60 a. *Fair linen* by Marie Westerman, Northfield, Minnesota, for Utica Lutheran Church, Mt. Sterling, Wisconsin. 1996. 8'7" x 22". Plain weave with warp wrapping. Linen. Fair linens need to be simple and functional. Although some churches dry-clean such textiles, many rely on altar guild members to take them home to launder. Therefore, they must be washable and bleachable. (Photograph by Fred Gonnerman)

61 a, b. *Altar cover* by Vera Gunter, Fort Lauderdale, Florida, for St. Eugene's Catholic Church, Asheville, North Carolina. 1996. 8' x 38". Linen weave, Brook's bouquet, twill. Pima cotton. This altar cloth for Lent is part of a set that includes a chasuble, and a wall hanging. The plum-purple was chosen to brighten the sanctuary, which is indirectly lit. The pastor of this church has commissioned local craftspersons to produce many items for the worship space, and the artist has made paraments in other colors as well. (Photograph by Tim Barnwell)

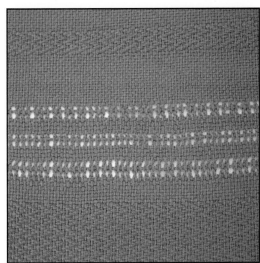

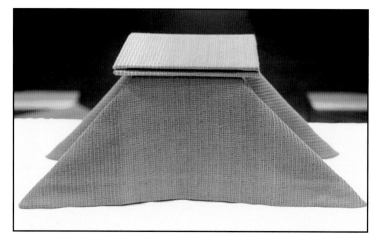

62. *Lenten veil and burse* by Mary Jane Thorne, Columbia, Missouri, for the Episcopal Church of St. Francis, Chapin, South Carolina. 1997. Burse is 9″ x 9″. Veil is 14″ x 14″. Three-shaft overshot. Cotton. Approximately 30 different purples, lavenders, and blues were shaded across the warp while two colors (purple and cobalt blue) were combined in the weft. The asymmetrical shading was chosen to complement other sanctuary textiles which are abstract in design. (Photograph by Pam Steude)

Veil and burse

Some traditions cover the communion elements with a chalice veil in white or the seasonal color. The veil is usually 20-24 inches square, but should be adjusted to the height of the chalice so that the veil will cover the chalice and touch, but not drape onto, the top of the altar. Fibers for the veil should allow for draping and yet be firm enough to hold the shape over the chalice. It is not necessary to line a chalice veil, but the outer corners should be substantial enough to hold a fold. The shape of the veil as it rests on the chalice is supported by a stiffened square called a pall.

The burse, an envelope of stiffened fabric consisting of two nine-inch squares hinged together, should match the veil. The burse holds the corporal, which is the cloth that covers the altar (on top of the fair linen) when the communion elements are placed on it.

Not all traditions use the veil and burse.

Tabernacle veil

Some Roman Catholic churches have a veil or curtain covering the door behind which the consecrated bread and wine are reserved. The colors of the curtain may be changed seasonally.

63 a. (lower left, facing page) *"I Am the Vine."* Tabernacle veil by Danita Ostasiewski McDonald, Greensboro, North Carolina, for Our Lady of Grace Church, Greensboro. 1994. 24″ x 14″(closed). Double weave pick-up. Three-strand embroidery cotton. This tabernacle veil consists of two identical panels. This design is an adaptation of a vine motif in the large mosaic which frames the sanctuary of this church. The vine has neither a beginning nor an end to symbolize the unity of the triune God.

63 b. (above) *Detail.* The variation in the green background layer closely matches the green marble inset into the white marble altar. Likewise the golds in the layer from which the vine is woven resemble gold marble set into the altar. (Photographs by John Skau)

Pulpit hangings

In many Protestant churches, the pulpit is a second central piece of furniture (along with the altar). The pulpit and the lectern (or reading stand) usually have paraments that match those for the altar.

Pulpit and lectern paraments are called falls. Pulpit and lectern falls need to be in proportion to the size of the piece of furniture. Avoid overpowering the furniture with weaving; covering about a third of the pulpit is a good starting point. Experiment with a piece of fabric or paper to determine a good size; make sure you look at it from a distance. In some churches, the pulpit fall may be a simpler version of the altar parament. The lectern hanging is sometimes simply a long bookmark.

If symbolism is used on the pulpit and lectern paraments, it should be in proportion to the size of the hanging and related to the theme of the altar paraments. Avoid repetition; look instead for complementary or analogous designs.

It is not necessary to cover the top of the reading stand or the pulpit. A hanging can cover only the front if it is fastened securely. A hook and loop fastening, such as Velcro®, is often used for this attachment.

In general the hook part of the fastening is attached to the pulpit and the loop to the parament. If the fastener is sewed first to a strip of cloth and then the cloth to the parament, the task of sewing will be easier. Never try to hang a textile directly onto the hook strip; the hooks will damage the textile by breaking the fibers.

64. *Pentecost paraments* by Susan Gustafson, Poplar, Wisconsin, for Grace Lutheran Church, Mora, Minnesota. 1985. 10" x 25" (longest dimension). Theo Moorman technique. Wool background with cotton, rayon, and metallic. The narrow sides of this pulpit presented a design challenge. The panels were woven sideways and then cut to fit the design. They were interlined with woven fusible interfacing and lined. The inlay technique allows textures and metallics to be visible well back in the nave. (Photograph by the artist)

65. (right) *Pulpit Fall for Ordinary Time* by Phyllis
Waggoner, Golden Valley, Minnesota, for Augsburg
College Chapel, Minneapolis. 1989. 60" x 15". 10/2
cotton. Damask on a draw loom. This chapel is
dominated by red brick, tan quarry tile, and natural
finished oak. A gridded oculus brings light into the
room; the grid is echoed in the chancel furniture. An
orderly arrangement of small lights in a three-tiered
ceiling complements the grid. The artist chose to use
this geometric grid as the theme upon which she did
five variations for five sets of paraments and stoles. The
parament colors are more intense than the natural
colors of the room, but they are all skewed to the
yellow/orange section of the color wheel. (Photograph
by the artist)

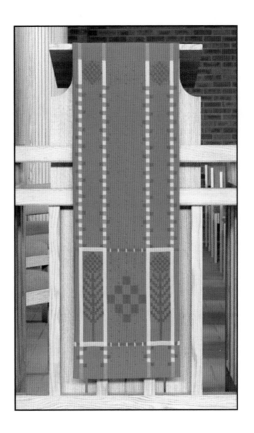

66 a. *Green pulpit fall* by Mary Elva Congleton Erf,
South Glastonbury, Connecticut, for the Congregational
Church of South Glastonbury. 1989. 33" x 21". Double
weave. 20/2 wool. The design of this pulpit fall was
inspired by the effect of stained glass windows with
colorful sections. The artist envisioned this design as a
large yellow-green cross shining through—off-center—
from behind. On the other hand, many parishioners
"see" the blue crosses formed by the outlines.

66 b. (below) *Dedication panel, green pulpit fall.* This
parament was given to the church by the artist in
memory of her father. She has given several paraments
to this church in memory of various family members.
(Photographs by Fred Gonnerman)

Designing and weaving for a sanctuary

The most important factor in designing for sanctuary furniture is taking accurate measurements. The exact height of any piece of furniture and the proportion of it that will be covered by the hanging are critical to the overall effect. Similarly the width of a hanging relative to the width of the furniture is a critical measurement. If a hanging is to lie across an altar or pulpit (rather than attach to the front), then the depth of the furniture should be measured as well.

Colors

Other factors to be considered in design are colors in other parts of the sanctuary and the shapes of the furniture.

Varying light conditions are possibly the most important factor. Light filtered through stained glass windows will affect the colors in the yarns, as will varying artificial light. Be sure to look at the yarns intended for the hangings in the sanctuary itself. If the interior of the sanctuary is sunny, the yarns you use should be colorfast. The motifs in the windows themselves are also a factor in the design. Perhaps the design for the weaving can refer to some of them.

Squaring the fabric

Fabric does not always come off the loom with perfect corners. Steam pressing may take care of this problem. A cutting board with squares printed on it will also help in the truing process.

The color of the furniture will also determine a direction for yarn tones. Marble or stone —whether off-white or black—will need to be addressed differently from wood. Even the weight of the woven piece should relate to the type of construction, in terms of how substantial it looks. Solid furniture needs a hanging of appropriate substance, while open furniture may need only minimal hangings.

The color of the floor and the walls will also influence the overall look of your weaving. If an altar stands in front of a brick wall, it will need a fairly striking design to offset the pattern in the brick.

Shape

The shape of the weaving for an altar or other sanctuary furniture depends on many factors besides the shape of the furniture. One important factor is what worshipers expect to see; the rectangular shape is the most common and conforms to what the loom naturally produces. Other shapes can be constructed from handwoven fabric, but the artist may have to educate the committee and the congregation to sell a unique design. Consider also how the hangings will be cared for and who will place them on the furniture as the seasons change. Sometimes an unusual shape works fine if it is placed by the person who wove it, while others find it difficult to install correctly.

Weaving

Paraments can be woven and constructed in many ways. A large hanging may be woven lengthwise, but hang crosswise. A seam joining two firm selvages is another way around the restrictions imposed by the width of a loom. A weaving that hangs down the front, goes over the top of a table, and continues down the back is a good solution for a free-standing altar. Or a linen or muslin panel can be attached on one edge of a handwoven panel to cover the top of the altar.

Planning the warp to make more than one item for a sanctuary setting is a wise use of time. With careful planning, a wide piece can be woven and then part of the warp taken off to make a narrow accompanying piece. It is even possible to drop a center portion of the warp to create two smaller pieces. If you plan to weave multiple units, make sure you plan adequate allowance for hems.

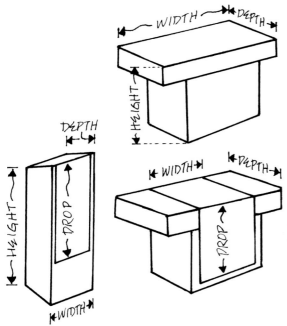

These drawings illustrate the dimensions that should be measured on a lectern or an altar before beginning the design of a hanging.

Construction of paraments

Catalog-made hangings for churches have linings and interlinings that keep them square and firm. Although this look may seem stiff, it is what churches expect. The handweaver must meet this challenge to produce work that is substantial and durable, hangs straight on the furniture, and holds up over a period of years. If a work sags, fades, or wears out quickly, it will discourage congregations from commissioning more handwoven work. Careful attention to construction is often the key to success; consider employing a seamstress if you do not sew.

Lined and interlined paraments can be constructed with the same methods used for the stole (see page 31). They may also be attached to a medium weight linen that covers the table or altar top.

The hem at the bottom of the hanging should not be obvious. Using a serger or iron-on interfacing can make the hem invisible. Narrow hems along the selvage edges will also help a parament to hang straight.

Attachment

How the hanging will be attached is another important part of design and construction. A common fastening device for an altar that is against the wall is a heavy bar placed in a sleeve along the back edge of the hanging. The sleeve may be the hem of the "skirt" or it may be a cloth sleeve attached to the edge of the handwoven material. Another common fastening device is a strip of Velcro® sewn to the edge of the weaving, matched by the "sticky back mate" fastened to the altar in an invisible place.

Storage

Storage requirements for handwoven work may be a necessary consideration during the design process. New storage cabinets for new hangings may or may not be feasible. When possible, handwoven work should be hung over padded rods. Another possibility is to roll the work on a padded cardboard tube. Handwoven work should never be folded.

The artist should provide care information at the time of delivery. This information should include the fiber content of the material, and pressing and dry-cleaning instructions. If the piece has been sprayed to resist moths and soil, the altar guild and the dry cleaner should be informed. This information will be helpful to the altar guild and can also be useful for insurance purposes.

Working with committees

Most designs for a sanctuary must be approved by a committee, even if they are being donated by the artist. Working with a committee gives the visual artist an opportunity to educate committee members about the nature of handwoven work, the names of the hangings, and their use according to the religious calendar. It is also an opportunity for the artist to listen to the ideas and concerns of the committee. A successful project should be satisfactory to the weaver and to the church so that the worship service is enhanced by handwoven work for many years to come.

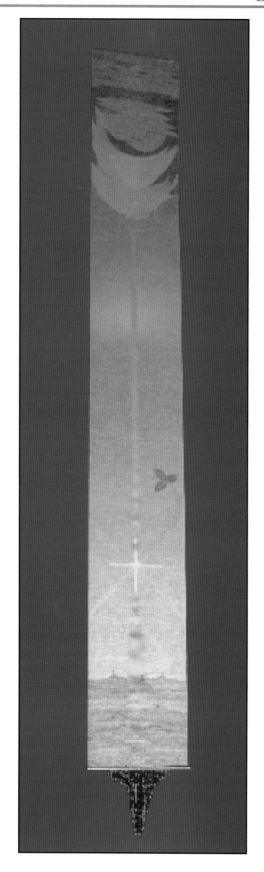

Baptismal hangings

If the baptismal font is included in the chancel furniture, small font hangings in the colors of the church year can also be designed for it. Some churches have a baptismal banner that hangs over the font. They may put it up only for baptisms, or they may leave it up all the time to emphasize the importance of the sacrament. If you are asked to design a hanging of this sort, you will probably be responsible for designing the hardware that supports it as well.

Hanging hardware should provide even support across the top edge of the textile, so that it will hang straight and flat. Materials used for hanging a textile should be compatible with the textile, so that they will not damage it. The hanging device should be inconspicuous, unless the hardware is intended to be a integral part of the design.

Of course, the easier it is to install and remove the textile, the better it will be maintained.

67. *Baptismal banner* by Lilla Larsen, Washougal, Washington for Washougal United Methodist Church. 1994. 144" X 19. Plain weave transparency. Linen, cotton, and wool. This piece combines several symbols of baptism and renewal, including the clouds which appear in the image of a dove, the cross which extends itself into a vine on the right, the light which is focused in the cross and then spreads across the water, and the beaded fringe which extends the water almost to the head of the person being baptized. The artist wove this banner with an outlined cartoon, but created the details as she was weaving. She had originally planned to have a plain fringe. The beaded fringe was an inspiration; she embroidered beads into the water to integrate the fringe into the piece. (Photograph by Thor Larsen)

Dossal

Some churches have a dossal or curtain behind the altar. (Sometimes it is called a reredos.) This curtain may be a permanent installation that affects the design of the altar hangings or it may be a design that changes with the seasons. If such an installation is in place or even contemplated, it should be taken into account in the design for any new parament. For additional information on mounting dossal curtains see pages 109–110.

68 a. (above) *Detail* of Easter tapestry. To emphasize the cross and make it appear to float forward, the artist used various shades of blue yarn in the center of the hanging so that the background appears to recede. She was so successful that many worshipers thought the cross and the hanging were two separate pieces when they first saw the tapestry. A close-up of the cross appears on the cover of this book. (Photographs by Marty Keeven)

68 b. *Easter tapestry* by Denise M. Mandel, St. Louis, Missouri, for the Basilica of St. Louis. 1996. 85" x 43". Weft-faced rug weave. Warp is linen; weft is rug wool. This weaving is the second in a series of tapestries by this artist for this sanctuary; she wanted to capture the spirit of the season while staying with her established format of borders that echo the mosaics in the chancel.

69. (left) *Altar cloth* by Jane Hartford, Santa Fe, New Mexico. Private collection. 1983. 90" x 26". Plain weave, twill, and rep. Cotton. Inspired by West African Kente cloth, this altar cloth was woven as seven narrow strips. The three 3¼-inch-wide mustard-colored strips were woven in plain weave with laid-in designs and stripes in twill weave. The deep red joining strips are in rep weave. The design was planned so that, when sewed together, the center became a focal point and the repeated designs, a larger pattern. The end of each 3-inch strip was woven in rep weave for one inch, completing a solid edge around the entire piece. Then each strip was divided into four plain weave tabs, 4 inches long and finished with 4-inch fringe. (Photograph by the artist)

70 a, b. (right) *Dossal* by Gloria Oldenburg, East Berlin, Pennsylvania, for Advent Lutheran Church, York, Pennsylvania. 1986. 96" x 72". Plain weave. Warp and weft are Harrisville shetland. This dossal was commissioned to hang behind the carved figure, which did not arrive until just a few days prior to the installation. To plan the design, the artist used a five-inch color photo of the carving. At first she intended to use an overshot pattern for the curtain, but found that the pattern design was lost from a distance and would detract from the carving. She then used plain weave and colors that would complement the carving. The piece was woven in two sections—one for the center and another, which was cut in half, for the sides. The pieces were washed before being sewed and hemmed with a decorative stitch. The curtain was professionally pressed and steamed. (Photographs by William J. Schintz)

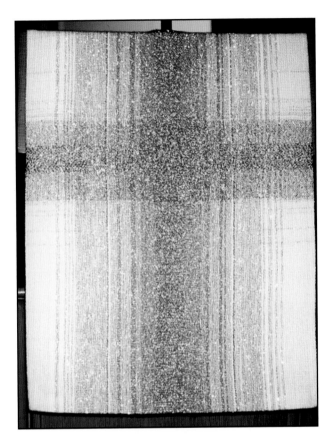

71. *Celebration pulpit fall* by Carol Droege, Grosse Pointe, Michigan, for First Presbyterian Church, Birmingham, Michigan. 1996. 19″ x 25″. Plain weave. Warp is 5/2 cotton with gold and rayon threads. Weft is Harrisville singles. This church has a large, simply decorated nave. The only indications of the church seasons are the pulpit and lectern falls. To be seen, these pieces had to be very bright, so as much gold as possible was worked into the piece. Additional red-gold was hand needled into the crossbar to get the desired effect of celebration and richness. (Photograph by the artist)

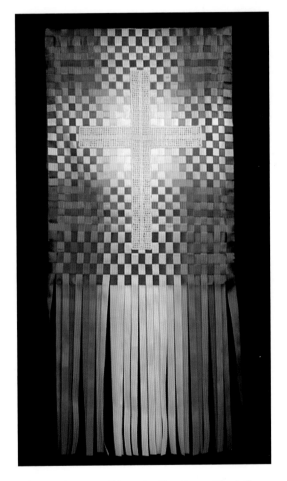

72. *Remembrance Ribbons* by Constance Hunt, San Francisco, California, for Temple United Methodist Church, San Francisco. 1987. 50″ x 17″. Interlacement. Ribbon, cotton, embroidery floss. This parament (and accompanying stoles, not shown) were created to illustrate a sermon series on remembering. The parament began with the vertical ribbons as the warp and the green ribbons as weft. Each week a few more ribbons were woven in to symbolize a time, a text, or a person being remembered that week. The crocheted cross, by Donna Decker, was appliquéed to the piece on the last Sunday. (Photograph by Gary Hunt)

FUNERAL PALLS

A funeral pall is the traditional covering for a casket. A pall should be full enough to cover the entire casket and the bier that it rests upon. An average casket is about 6 feet long by 19 inches wide by 15 inches deep. White is often recommended for funeral palls, although purple and black were formerly used.

Although palls available through church catalogue houses may be lined or have fringe, a well-designed handwoven pall can have a plain hem and no lining.

A complementary orphrey in the form of a cross is an accepted way of covering a center seam. The orphrey may be joined at the center with a mitered seam.

74. *Funeral pall* in three panels by Catherine Leary, SSJ, Springfield, Massachusetts, for the Motherhouse of the Sisters of St. Joseph, Holyoke, Massachusetts. 1995. 144" x 90". Eight-shaft three-block crackle. Silk. This pall consists of three equal-width panels, joined so as to meet at the angle where the coffin top meets its sides. The center panel is entirely in a cruciform pattern weave. The two side panels are—in order, one-third plain weave, one-third pattern, and one-third plain weave. When the three sections are sewed together, the arrangement of pattern weave forms a large cross. The artist hemmed the pall on a coffin so that the corners would fall smoothly and hang lower than the straight edges. This pall was designed specifically for the chapel of the Motherhouse; its structure assures that the crosses of the pattern weave are visible no matter where one sits in the chapel. (Photograph by Larry Grenier)

73. *Funeral pall* by Jennae R. Giles, Mohall, North Dakota, for Good Shepherd Lutheran Church, Ashland, Wisconsin. 1985. 12' x 8'. Inlay overshot. 20/2 wool/silk with a 50/50 blend of metallic gold for the cross. This pall was woven in three sections. The artist has taken the Blooming Leaf overshot motif illustrated in this photograph as her trademark. (Photograph courtesy of the artist)

75. *Funeral pall* by Joyce Harter for St. Ansgar's Lutheran Church, Cannon Falls, Minnesota. 12′ x 6′. Four-shaft double weave, open at one side. Textured rayon and wool. This funeral pall is in plain weave, as a single fabric twice the warp width, with the cross form on the fold edge of the warp. The single width of the warp was 45″, to allow for shrinkage and a hem. The artist achieved a cross form by warping the color band down the center of the long warp and crossing it in the weft. The large piece is difficult to steam press alone, so it was professionally steam pressed at a reputable dry cleaner. A funeral director advised rounded corners so that they would not be in the way for rolling a casket. The artist made a cardboard template for cutting and then steam-shaping the corners. She turned the selvages to form the hem on the sides. She serged the hem in matching thread and then worked a hemstitched edge by hand around the entire 32 feet of the circumference. This detail gives the pall a picot edge. The cross form lies beautifully across the top of a casket. The white of the funeral pall is symbolic of the white gown often worn for Christian baptism. (Photograph by Fred Gonnerman)

76. *Rachel's tallit* by Steven Medwin, Broomall, Pennsylvania. Artist's collection. 1996. 60" x 8". Sixteen-shaft point twill with inlay. Cotton with rayon inlay. This tallit was woven for the Bat Mitzvah of the artist's daughter. He combined inlay techniques with the diamond pattern of the rest of the tallit. Typically the neckband *(atarah)* is sewed on separately, but the artist wanted to eliminate bulk and so incorporated it into the design. (Photograph by Roxy Schiavone)

Chapter 6
WEAVING A TALLIT

Paula Stewart

77. *Traditional prayer shawl* by Paula Stewart. Privately owned. 1994. 78" x 31". (Bag is 9" x 11"). Monk's belt. Wool with metallic accents. This traditional prayer shawl has a matching bag and *kippah* (skullcap). It is part of a family collection of prayer shawls, in which each of four sons selected a style and color that reflected his individuality. (Photo by Stanton Willins)

IN MY FIRST YEARS of weaving, I explored. I tried clothing; I tried upholstery; I tried rugs; I tried table linens; I just kept trying. I envied those who were able to focus on a single facet of weaving; their work had a direction and a vision. Paradoxically, while I was making these observations, my weaving began to evolve and take on an identity of its own; one recurring theme in my work was Jewish liturgical weaving.

In the beginning, I wove a prayer shawl (*tallit*) and now, years later, I still weave prayer shawls *(tallitot)*. Somehow, whether it is a new aspect to perfect or a new design to try, the weaving of tallitot keeps drawing me back spiritually.

My liturgical handweaving reflects my Jewish heritage. Weaving Judaism into my cloth is a reminder of who I am. It is fulfilling for me as a weaver; it is also a spiritual bridge between faith and form. It allows me to experience my faith in a form other than the worship service.

A tallit is a shawl of honor and an outward declaration of faith. The rabbi and cantor of the synagogue sometimes wear a tallit when conducting a service. A tallit is also worn by the individual called to read from the Torah (scrolls). A tallit is worn by adults over the age of thirteen during morning prayers and on Yom Kippur (the Day of Atonement). Sometimes Jews are buried in their personal tallit.

An individual is not required to own a tallit. If a worshiper doesn't have one, the synagogue offers a supply of prayer shawls near the entrance to the sanctuary for use during service. However, most adult males like to have their own, and it is becoming common for women to own a personal tallit as well. Traditionally, the parents present a tallit at the Bar/Bat Mitzvah (son/daughter of commandment) at the age of thirteen. It is a visible sign of adulthood in the Jewish community. Recently, it has become popular to create a personal tallit as an individual statement of personality and values. This trend is evidenced by the variety of colors and designs in the prayer shawls worn by worshipers.

Traditional tallitot

For the purposes of this discussion, I have focused on the traditional tallit worn for worship. Most often it is white with black or blue stripes and made of wool, cotton, or silk. Some fibers may not be mixed. The Torah specifically prohibits the mixing of wool and linen, although it is all right to mix silk with anything or to have a tallit of all wool or all linen. The Torah says, "Thou shalt not sow thy field with two kinds of seed; nor shall there come upon thee a garment of two kinds of stuff mingled together." (Leviticus 19:19)* This prohibition is called *shatnez*.

An average-sized tallit measures two feet by six feet but can vary depending upon the person wearing the garment. The main body of the tallit needs to be a sett that will allow a soft, draping look. I tend to choose fine threads (18/2) with close setts (24-30 e.p.i.) that will give a lightweight fabric comfortable for the wearer.

(Text continues on page 80)

*All scripture citations in this section are taken from *Pentateuch & Haftorahs* by Dr. J.H. Hertz.

78. *Tallit* by Moocho Scott Salomon, Bethlehem, New Hampshire. 1995. 74½" x 22". Overshot variations and supplementary warp pick-up. Cotton and silk. Although the pattern used here is a well-known overshot pattern (Kirschbaum's #4 from *Handweaver's Pattern Book* by Marguerite Davison), the artist has used variations such as weaving on opposites and in the Italian manner. Leno has also been incorporated. It has been customary in the Jewish tradition to weave a tallit in white with black or blue stripes. This tallit breaks away from traditional colors. The *atarah* (neckband) reads "How precious is your kindness, Lord; the sons of men seek refuge in the shadow of your wings." Two variations of the skullcap are present: traditional and pillbox styles. (Photograph by Tom Long)

TYING TZITZIT

And the Lord spoke unto Moses saying, "Speak unto the children of Israel, and bid them that they make them throughout their generations fringes in the corners of their garments, and that they put with the fringe of each corner a thread of blue. And it shall be unto you for a fringe, that ye may look upon it, and remember all the commandments of the Lord, and do them…" Numbers 15:37-40

There are at least two schools of thought on tying the *tzitzit* (fringe). One is that only a rabbi should tie the tzitzit; the other is that it is a good deed *(mitzvah)* for the wearer to tie them personally. If you are going to tie them yourself, the following instructions will be helpful.

A hole for the tzitzit is made approximately two inches from the corner of the cloth; it is finished like a buttonhole to keep the hole from tearing or fraying. Most authorities recommend buying a set of tzitzit from a local Hebrew book store or a synagogue gift shop. Look for a rabbinical certification tag on the set of strings to ensure the threads were spun for the purpose of being tzitzit thread.

Open the set of tzitzit; four of the threads will be longer and are usually wrapped around the other twelve in the package. Separate the threads into four groups; put one long thread in each group. The long thread is called the *shamesh* or servant string and is wound around the three shorter threads in each corner.

Take a group of four strands and pull it through one of the corner holes. Adjust the threads so they are even except for the one side where the *shamesh* thread will be longer. At this point you have doubled the threads giving you eight. Here you should stop

and say, "I am doing this to fulfill the commandment of tzitzit" (*lashem mitzvot tzitzit*). Then with four threads in each hand make a double knot. Take the *shamesh* and wind it exactly seven times around the other seven strands. Make seven complete winds. Make another double knot (four strands over four). Then make eight windings with the *shamesh,* and another double knot. Eleven windings and another double knot. Thirteen windings and the final double knot. This completes one tzitzit. Some interpreters say that the the tzitzit in the four corners of the tallit represent the presence of the Lord in the four corners of the world.

Generally, the thread of blue that was originally part of the tzitzit is not used since the ancient source of the blue color is no longer available. Many tallitot are woven with blue stripes to serve as a reminder of the blue thread. According to tradition, the blue dye was extracted from a hilazon, a Mediterranean species of snail which is thought to be extinct. All white tzitzit are commonly used, although some contemporary Jews have reintroduced the old practice of a blue thread.*

* Recently, Reuven Praeger of Jerusalem has announced that he has a legitimate source of the ancient blue dye and has begun to market tzitzit which contain the blue thread. Praeger's address is listed in the source appendix.

Drawing by Marie Westerman

79. *Bat Mitzvah tallit* by Paula Stewart. Private collection. 1995. 72" x 13½". Undulating twill. Silk with metallic and beads. This is a feminine interpretation of the prayer shawl traditionally worn by males. A drawstring bag, pillbox-shaped hat, and embroidered blessing all complement the Bat Mitzvah theme. The beading and the wearer's Hebrew name embellished on this piece were requested by the owner. (Photograph by Images by Floom)

Color and design are open to interpretation. The traditional and the contemporary are both acceptable. A tallit may be decorated with lettering or with any other respectful embellishment.

A tallit is fringed on both ends and has a special set of fringes known as tzitzit (see page 79) in each corner. The tzitzit are knotted and wrapped in a precise manner; they make a simple rectangular piece of cloth into a prayer shawl.

Another part of the tallit is the *atarah* (collar/crown) which appears in the center on one edge. This area serves as a reference point to the wearer for the correct positioning of the prayer shawl. Although an *atarah* is not required, it is usually included in the piece. The design can be decorative or it can incorporate the traditional Hebrew benediction—a prayer of thanks for the commandment to wear the tzitzit—that is

recited before putting on a tallit. Some weavers make an *atarah* by weaving it in as part of the material. More often it is woven separately and sewed on when finishing. If an *atarah* is to be woven separately, extra material can also be made for small corner squares where the tzitzit are to be placed. This gives the material some stability around the hole and draws attention to the special nature of the tzitzit.

Two companion pieces

Two companion pieces to the tallit are the *kippah* (skullcap) and a bag to hold both the tallit and the *kippah*. A flat rectangular bag approximately 10" x 12" (finished size) with a zipper on top will hold the tallit and *kippah*. The design on the bag often matches the prayer shawl. Lining for the bag and *kippah* is optional but it gives a finished look.

The *kippah* or skullcap must be worn by men, and is increasingly worn by women, as a sign of respect during services. Even non-Jews entering the sanctuary are asked to cover their heads with a "house" *kippah* as a sign of respect. The *kippah* is sometimes viewed as a sign of piety; some people wear a *kippah* at all times. More recently, the *kippah* has become a symbol of Jewish identity. The color or the style of a *kippah* can be an indication of political preference.

The small, round crocheted *kippah* is an Israeli style; the satin, pieced *kippah* is widely worn in the United States; the latest *kippah* fashion is the pillbox-shaped Moroccan style. Variations of these basic styles are limitless. White is the traditional color for weddings and for the High Holy Days whereas black is worn at daily services as well as funerals. A *kippah* can be made of nearly any material—suede, velvet, satin or something handwoven—and in nearly any color or form.

Naturally, if the *kippah* is being made to coordinate with a tallit or a special event, then those elements will influence the design. Customize the fit for a finished look. Although standard-sized *kippah* are sold commercially, people do not have standard-sized heads and most likely have a preference for what is comfortable. Measure what the recipient is currently wearing for worship and ask about its fit. Make adjustments to accommodate individual taste. The wearer will appreciate the attention and service that a one-of-a-kind piece requires. (*A pattern for a* kippah *can be found on page 145.*)

As with other handwoven garments, it is wise to give your client care instructions for the tallit and the *kippah*. It should be kept in the bag and dry-cleaned periodically by a reputable cleaner.

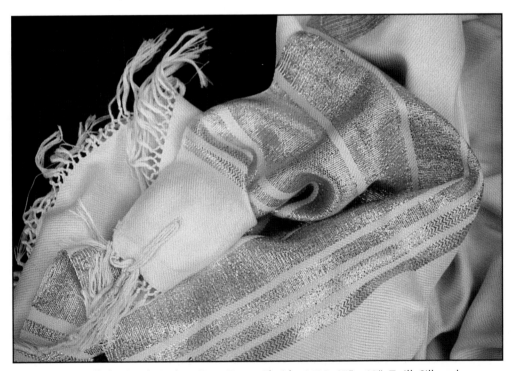

80. *Woman's tallit* by Candy Barbag, Boca Raton, Florida. 1992. 67" x 19". Twill. Silk and metallic. This off-white and gold tallit was woven by the artist to wear at her son's Bar Mitzvah. She chose neutral colors so that it could be worn on many occasions. This tallit has been loaned to friends to wear when they join their children at the Torah on the occasion of their Bar/Bat Mitzvahs. (Photograph by Jan Miller)

TO WEAVE A TALLIT

*A tallit is a rectangle with fringes on the non-sel-
vage ends. Ritual fringes called tzitzit are tied into
the four corners in accordance with Biblical law. A
tallit is customarily woven in one piece. By tradition
a neck piece is either incorporated into or added to
the weaving. Otherwise there are few design restrictions—and room for much creativity—in making a
tallit.*

Design considerations

Two obvious design considerations are the size
of the individual and personal preference for a
particular style. There is no one size for a tallit,
but the usual dimensions are 18 to 48 inches
wide and 72 inches long. In the case of a
Bar/Bat Mitzvah commission, consider making
the prayer shawl proportional to the wearer's
adult growth potential. Though the garment
may appear oversized on a thirteen-year old
body, it is impractical to do anything else.

Decide on the pattern or design elements to
be incorporated into the tallit. An individual
may personalize a prayer shawl with a favorite
color, prayer, or vision. Often the main body of
the shawl is plain weave and the striping is colored or patterned with an overshot or inlaid
design. Avoid patterns with long floats. A
prayer shawl is unlined and long floats can easily catch on clothing or jewelry.

The suggested dimensions and traditional
designs are spatial directions rather than an
exact pattern. New interpretations of this very
traditional garment are often the welcome
result of talent and creativity.

Fiber

The tallit is most often white or off-white and
made of wool, cotton, or silk. Synthetic materials are also acceptable, but not usually the fiber
of choice. Remember the prohibition against
mixing wool and linen when choosing fibers. A
fine 18/2 or 20/2 wool or silk, sett at 24–30 e.p.i,
makes an excellent choice for warp. The same
fiber can be used in the weft for a soft drapable
fabric. Many weavers use color or novelty
threads for the striping, collar *(atarah),* or corners. Choose colors that are colorfast and
compatible to avoid finishing surprises later.

Warp

Calculate enough warp to include four to eight
inches of fringe on each end. Add enough material for a matching *kippah* requiring six
triangular shapes (4 inches at the base and 5
inches in height including a ¼-inch seam
allowance). Add also the material for a 10 x 12
inch bag (two pieces, each 11 x 14 inches, including a ½-inch seam allowance). *(A pattern for a
kippah can be found on page 145.)* Extra material
for corner reinforcements is optional.

These directions assume that the weaver has
sampled the materials, knows how much warp
to allow for shrinkage in finishing, and has
allowed for loom waste in calculating the warp.

Prepare a warp and dress the loom. Take the
time to check the threading for accuracy and
correct any errors. Quite often weavers put on
enough warp for multiple tallit sets in order to
save preparation time. It is more efficient and
increases productivity.

Weaving

Weave a heading to assure that the warp
threads are evenly spaced and to check the pattern and choice of sett. Small adjustments at
this stage often make the difference between a
hastily produced piece and one that is professional looking. Remember to leave enough
warp for fringe at the beginning of the body of
the tallit. Start by weaving four inches of plain
weave to accommodate the corner reinforce-
ment patches whether they are woven into the
cloth or attached to it afterward. There will be

two corners at the beginning of the tallit, one on the left and one on the right side of the garment. This same process will be repeated on the other end of the shawl to create a total of four corners.

After the corners are done, any color or pattern may be applied to the rest of the shawl. Stripes may be of any size, shape, or color. Black stripes and blue thread stripes are traditional. The Star of David and a seven-branch menorah are also traditional designs.

The only other design element that needs to be considered is the collar *(atarah)*. The collar should work with the rest of the weaving, but it may be woven as part of the tallit or it may be applied as part of the finishing. Make it long enough to be seen around the wearer's neck for

at least 20 inches. Some weavers choose to make the collar piece extend the full length of the shawl, from corner to corner. More commonly it is a 20- to 26-inch strip of cloth, two to four inches wide, added to the finished tallit.

If the collar will be a separate piece of cloth attached as part of the finishing, then the main body of the shawl can be completed in plain or patterned weaving. If inlaid lettering or an inlaid pattern is part of the collar design, then deciding where to start the lettering will be a design consideration. The tallit benediction is a traditional design on this collar. Letters or designs should be graphed to make sure they fit the intended space.

When a tallit is woven in plain weave, as many are, it is important to keep the beat con-

81. *Bar Mitzvah tallit* by Paula Stewart. Private collection. 1991. 78" x 33". Summer and winter. Wool with metallic. This Bar Mitzvah tallit set has a connecting Star of David design and triple-knotted fringe. (Photograph by Images by Floom)

sistent. Pay particular attention to the selvages of the fabric since the edges of the tallit are visible. Splice the ends of the fibers smoothly to avoid the appearance of a mistake in the weaving. Be especially careful with the edges of inlaid work.

When the tallit is its full length (measured with the tension off) with an allowance for shrinkage, add on another four to eight inches for fringe.

Material for a *kippah*, a bag, corner reinforcements, and a collar can be woven on the same warp. On average, these additions require an extra yard of fabric. Although the collar and the corners will remain flat when they are sewed on the shawl, the bag and the *kippah* will be cut and pieced into three-dimensional shapes. It will help to draw the sections of a *kippah* and a tallit bag on paper; lay the paper on the fabric before it is cut from the loom. Again remember to allow for shrinkage when the fabric is finished.

Finishing

Take the cloth off the loom. Cut the tallit apart from the rest of the woven pieces. Knot the tallit fringes at both ends. Fringes can be simple or fancy; an easy overhand knot is common, but more elaborate treatments add a personal touch. Wash the tallit and the extra cloth in the washing machine with a mild detergent and cold water. Washing handwoven cloth in a washing machine can be scary, but the results are quite beautiful. Press it with an iron until the fabric feels dry to the touch. Although it takes a long time to dry fabric this way, the results are much smoother than if the fabric is dried, even briefly, in the dryer. (A dryer may set wrinkles so that they cannot be pressed out.)

When the fabric is dry on the surface, hang it over a shower rod or a door to finish drying overnight. The next day it will be ready to cut and sew.

There are really no assemblage rules for the pieces of the tallit set. Selvages on the prayer shawl can be left as is, or they can have a narrow rolled edge that is serged for a finished look. Collars and corners can be machine or hand stitched on the tallit. Once the construction details are complete, all that is needed are the tzitzit (fringe) to transform this shawl into a ritual garment. Instructions for tying the tzitzit are included in the text of this chapter. (See page 79.)

The *kippah* and the bag are usually lined with a cotton or non-slippery fabric. This lining is especially important to keep the skullcap in place without hairpins. The bag used to carry the tallit and *kippah* usually closes with a zipper. Some bags use buttons, snaps, Velcro®, or drawstrings, but zippers are generally the first choice.

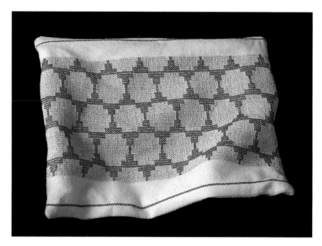

82. *Star of David tallit bag* by Paula Stewart. Detail of plate 81. The bag is 9″ x 11″ and closes with a zipper. (Photograph by Images by Floom)

84. *Tallit* by Moocho Scott Salomon, Bethlehem, New Hampshire. 1993. 80" x 45". Summer and winter polychrome weave. Wool and Lurex. The artist chose summer and winter polychrome for this tallit because she wanted strong, pure colored stripes without halftones. The full spectrum of colors is emphasized by the juxtaposition of black. The vertically woven Star of David creates a flow off the shoulders when the tallit is worn in the traditional manner as shown here. (Photograph by David Adam)

83. *"Division of the waters—Day 2."* Tallit by Marcia Wiener, Port Jefferson, New York, for Jacob Bigeleisen. 1983. 70" x 27". Plain weave and twill basket weave. Wool. The artist has chosen the biblical theme of creation—"in the beginning"—for the design elements of her woven tallitot. Using sequences of color to form "light," "darkness," "heavens," "earth," "sea," and so forth, each day of creation is depicted. (Photograph by the artist)

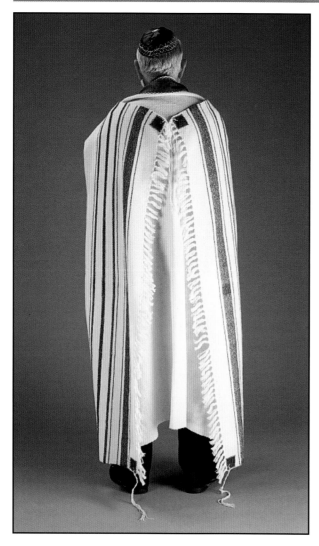

86. *Tallit* by Nancy Goodman, St. Paul, Minnesota. 1996. 76" x 20". Plain weave. Silk/wool. This piece was designed for a 13-year old boy preparing for his Bar Mitzvah. Once the design was chosen he had a large part in picking the colors that he wanted. (Photograph by Richard Danor)

85. *Tallit* by Laura-Lee Karp Tolliver, Seattle, Washington. Collection of the artist. 1989. 75½" plus fringe x 57". Plain weave. Wool. This tallit is of the size and color traditionally donned by Orthodox men during Sabbath and High Holy Day services in the synagogue. Less traditional are the *atarah* (neckband) and a silk lining in the shoulder area. These, along with the corners of the garment, are embellished with the style of embroidery brought to Israel by Yemenite Jews. The artist uses this style of embroidery in memory of her grandmother. (Photograph by Roger Schreiber)

88. *Tallit* by Jill Peek and Laurie Gross, Santa Barbara, California. 72" x 45". First produced in 1987. Extended point twill and ikat rep weave. 20/2 cotton. This contemporary interpretation of a traditional Jewish prayer shawl utilizes an ikat band as its central design motif. The ikat band functions as the *atarah* or collar area where one often finds the words of the prayer that is said when one is putting on the tallit. (Photograph by Marvin Rand)

87. Atarah *on a tallit for a "Klezmer Cantor"* by Roz Houseknecht, Rockville, Maryland. 1995. 80" x 40". Plain weave; stripes in basket weave. Cotton, silk, metallic. This tallit was designed to present as a gift to a man who loves bold colors and the excitement of Klezmer music. The artist played a tape of a Klezmer band to inspire the design. The *atarah* was created with a supplementary weft in a stair step pattern. (Photograph by the artist)

Using the Hebrew Alphabet

Using Hebrew words to personalize a tallit or other ritual textile is a wonderful way to individualize weaving. A blessing can be inlaid or embroidered along the *atarah* or the names of the tallit weaver can be incorporated into the tzitzit reinforcements. Ritual blessings can be woven into a challah cover or a Passover linen. However, using Hebrew words and letters is a special challenge in any craft. If the weaver is not a native speaker of Hebrew, it is wise to have the planned words proofread by a rabbi to avoid misspellings and inadvertent wrong meanings.

After the words are proofread, pick a style of lettering that does justice to the handwork. Many lovely pieces are spoiled by amateur lettering. Calligraphic Hebrew alphabets that have been graphed for needlepoint are especially useful for the handweaver. Sources for such alphabets are listed in the bibliography. *The Art of Judaic Needlework* by Ita Aber is especially good.

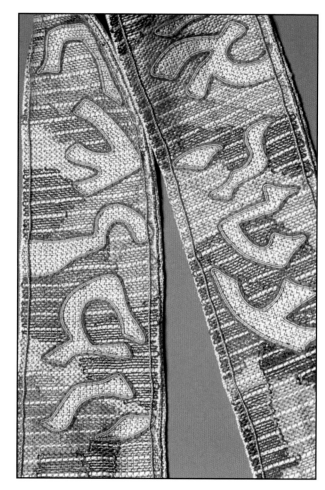

89. *Robe of Light, detail of atarah* by Ina Golub, Mountainside, New Jersey, for Rabbi Richard A. Block. 1994. Theo Moorman technique. Silk. This tallit was inspired by a phrase from Psalm 104: 1-2, "You are clothed in glory and majesty, wrapped in a robe of light." These words, selected by Rabbi Block, inspired the gradated, light-filled colors with abstract shapes representing light that embellish this tallit. The Hebrew letters were transcribed freehand in a calligraphic style for reproduction in the Moorman technique. (Photograph by Taylor Photo)

90. *"Joseph's Colors"* tallit, detail of *atarah*, by Roz Houseknecht, Rockville, Maryland. 1996. 72" x 25". Block weave. Silk. Attached *atarah* with cotton and metallic embroidery. The artist photocopied the desired text and then transcribed it on paper for spacing. She then transferred the lettering to handwoven fabric by using a marker on a light box. The marked letters were then embroidered with pearl cotton. The customer was part of an adult Bat Mitzvah class and wanted a tallit that would reflect her joy and commitment to studying. The text reads "When the ram's horn sounds a long blast, they may go up on the mountain." (Photograph by the artist)

91. *Keith's tallit* by Candy Barbag, Boca Raton, Florida. 1996. 72" x 41½". Rosepath. Silk and metallic. This tallit was woven for the artist's son. He chose the colors of the rainbow. The picture shows a detail of the *atarah,* where the Hebrew names of the artist and her husband are written. The names were first written out on paper, then passed through an optical scanner for a sewing machine which converted the names into embroidery on a piece of plain weave fabric. This fabric was then stitched to the neck of the tallit. (Photograph by Jan E. Miller)

92 a, b. *Torah covers and curtain with valance* by Pinky (Hermana) Shmerler, Cherry Hill, New Jersey, for Temple Israel, Norfolk, Virginia. 1994-1995. Curtain 90" x 90". Torah covers vary in size. Basket weave with tapestry inlay and plain weave. Wool. The Torah mantles, which were fabricated to cover the Torah scrolls, have tapestry design inlays in black, cobalt, garnet, aubergine, and gold. The colors were chosen to complement the tapestry design in the ark curtains and the valance. (Photographs by Ramon Photography Studio)

Chapter 7
OTHER JUDAIC TEXTILES
by Paula Stewart

93. *Torah Mantles* by Paula Stewart for Robison Jewish Home Chapel, Portland, Oregon. 1993. Left 30" x 32"; Right 21" x 32". Summer and winter. Silk. These coordinated Torah covers were customized to fit the different-sized Torah scrolls. Subtle color shadings, enhanced by piping details, add interest. (Photograph by Stanton Willins)

THE TRADITIONS OF Jewish life are historical and varied. Connection with the past and continuing interaction with the present provide numerous opportunities for weavers to create ritual textiles for use in the home and in the synagogue. Although many weavers concentrate on making *tallitot*, as described in the preceding chapter, others make ritual textiles of several levels of complexity. These less common textiles are described in this chapter.

Challah cover

Making ritual cloth to be used by family or friends is a non-threatening way to begin a spiritual exploration. For example, the weekly Sabbath includes a special Friday night dinner that encourages the use of table linens. The traditional braided bread (challah) is often covered by a small rectangular or circular cloth inscribed with the words *Shabbat Shalom* (Sabbath peace) in Hebrew letters. A tradition says that the bread is covered so that it will not be offended when the wine is blessed first during the Sabbath meal ritual.

A challah cover is manageable as a first project in ritual textiles; no exact shape or size is required, nor are there design restrictions. The cover only needs to be large enough to cover the bread it is intended for; decorations may reflect personal aesthetics or preference. Of course a challah cover should be easy to wash and be pleasant to see at the weekly Sabbath table.

Passover textiles

A weaver might also begin by creating a series of linens for specific use during Passover. Annually—in the Hebrew month of Nisan—Jews commemorate the Exodus out of the land of Egypt during the festival of *Pesach* (Passover). The word *Pesach* literally means "pass over"; it refers to the story in Exodus 13 when the angel of death killed the firstborn of the Egyptian families and passed over the

HOME TEXTILES

94. *Matzoh cover "Aviv"* by Roz Houseknecht, Rockville, Maryland. 1993. 13" x 13". Thousand Flowers. Cotton. The weave structure (from *Handweaver's Pattern Book* by Marguerite Davison) was chosen to represent the flowers of spring. This cover is one of a series woven on the same warp; each has a different "garden of flowers." The lettering is done with chain stitch embroidery. (Photograph by the artist)

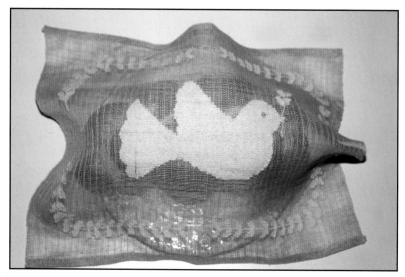

95. *Dove challah cover* by Carol Bodin, Columbia, Maryland. Privately owned. 1987. 14" x 17". Scandinavian transparency. Natural linen. The artist, who has long been fascinated with transparency techniques, wanted to see if she could create a challah cover through which the bread, which is very important to the Sabbath meal, would be visible. The piece needs to be handled carefully in washing. The appearance of texture in plain weave was achieved by denting every fourth and fifth thread together. (Photograph by Kim Bodin)

homes of the Israelites, which had been marked on the door posts with the blood of a lamb. After the plagues, the Egyptians let the Israelites go.

During the flight to freedom, there was no time to wait for bread to rise, so a flat bread, called matzoh, was carried and eaten by the Israelites. Therefore, during the Passover holiday, it is forbidden to eat leavened bread. An important part of the Passover ritual is to rid the house of all leavened foods and objects that have been used with these foods. Toasters and bread boxes, for example, are put away for this eight-day period of celebration. Many people have special table linens used only for Passover. What fine motivation for more weaving! Passover pillows, hand towels, matzoh covers, table linens, and perhaps special *kippot* are all possible.

The Passover service—called a Seder—is conducted at home around the dining room table. *Seder* means "order" and is read from a book known as the Haggadah. The leader of the Seder has a cushion at his or her seat; reclining during the service is a symbol of freedom. (A person who is no longer a slave can choose to recline or sit tall while eating a meal.) A Passover pillow can either be a woven cloth cut and pieced together with a removable cushion insert, or it can be a pillow cover designed to be used on any available pillow in the house. Once again, as with most other Passover textiles, this item needs to be woven of fibers that can be washed, and stored for most of the year.

Part of the Seder is ritual hand washing, imitating the priestly practices of ancient times; hand washing symbolizes the purification of the Passover participants. Naturally, the act of hand washing necessitates a hand towel. A Passover hand towel can vary in size and design, but the cloth will need to be practical. It will get wet when it is used by several people, but it is an object that is used only for the

Seders, two nights a year. (In the western hemisphere, Seders are celebrated on two consecutive nights in order to make sure that one will coincide with the celebration in Jerusalem.)

The unleavened bread (matzoh) is an important part of the Seder table and can be displayed in a variety of ways. A cloth matzoh cover can be placed over the tray containing the matzoh; sometimes a three-pocket bag is used for the matzohs themselves. The three *matzoth* are referred to in the Seder service. To make a matzoh bag the weaver needs to measure the size of the matzoh (approximately 6½" x 7") and allow for the fact that the bag will sit directly on the food table. The Hebrew word for matzoh or for Passover can be inlaid in the weaving or can be embellished on the cloth as part of the finishing.

The Passover plate contains six food items— parsley, egg, lettuce, bitter herbs, shankbone, and *haroset**—symbolizing parts of the story of the Exodus. These items can be inspiration for Passover designs; use the shapes and colors found in eggs, apples, walnuts, and greens. Traditions vary among households and geographic locations, but wine cups, grapes, vines, figs, dates, or popular spring themes such as trees and flowers are also appropriate Passover motifs. In making Seder linens, choose colors wisely and avoid fibers that are hard to clean. Think about storage and how to maintain a fresh look each year.

These projects might be considered for beginning Jewish ritual weaving. Master the smaller, simple weavings for your family or friends before branching out to the local Jewish community or the world at large.

---

*Haroset (derived from *heres* meaning "clay") is usually represented by a mixture of apples, nuts, and wine. The texture and color are intended to call to mind the bricks the slaves made for Pharaoh.

96. *Chuppah "Ani L'dodi"* by Phyllis Kantor, Eugene, Oregon, for Temple Sinai, Champaign, Illinois. Calligraphy by Reeva Kimble; wooden frame by Charles Marpet. 1993. 7'6" high by 72" square. Theo Moorman technique on 16 shafts. Silk and cotton. Embellished with velvet, pearls, and semi-precious beads. The name of this piece is taken from the Song of Songs. ("I am my beloved's and my beloved is mine." 2:16.) The *chuppah* is designed so that the front upper piece and the large backdrop hang on a wall when it is not in use. The fabric attaches to this frame with Velcro® and to the wall frame the same way. The border on the back of the piece compensates for the fact that it was impossible to weave a piece 72 inches wide. The border is velvet. (Photograph by Kent Peterson)

Chuppah

On a slightly larger scale, the *chuppah* (wedding canopy) is a popular article to weave. The *chuppah*, under which the marriage ceremony takes place, can be used in a synagogue, a private home, or a rented space, as well as outdoors. It is supported by a frame or by poles; it will vary in size—generally extending a few inches over the sides of the frame to give the impression of a tent. Symbolically, entering into the *chuppah* or standing under it is a reference to the home the new couple will share. (Sometimes a couple will use a personal tallit as a *chuppah*.)

97. *Wedding tallit* by Jeanne Heifetz, New York, New York, for the wedding of Cindy Siegel and Peter Kupfer. 1991. 7' x 3'. Plain weave with twill stripes. Cotton and silk warp, silk weft. The bride and groom used the Sephardic custom of wrapping themselves in a single tallit during the ceremony. Since the artist knew the tallit would be seen from behind, she chose warp stripes rather than the more traditional weft stripes. After the tallit was finished, the bride, the groom, and the artist met to tie the *tzitzit,* so they could participate in the transformation of the weaving from cloth to ritual garment. (Photograph by Jonathan Bumas)

The *chuppah* only needs to be large enough to cover the couple during the ceremony. Normally the installation is temporary and a good design will reflect these criteria. Many synagogues have a wedding canopy which has been custom-designed to meet their specifications; they display this item as a wall hanging when it is not in use for a ceremony. If a *chuppah* is to serve this dual function, it must be planned to be viewed in more than one dimension. Likewise, if a couple decides to make a personal *chuppah,* it can also be used for a wall hanging or a bed canopy in the home. While there are no Biblical instructions regarding the fibers in a *chuppah,* it is probably wise not to mix fibers rather than risk offending someone. White is often chosen as the color for a *chuppah,* but this choice is a personal preference. The canopy design can include symbols such as doves, pomegranates, and other evocations of eternal love and perfection.

Elijah's chair

Another item that may be used either in a synagogue or a home is an "Elijah's Chair"—a chair used for baby-naming ceremonies or a circumcision. Jews believe that the Prophet Elijah is present at each circumcision to bear witness to Israel's loyalty to the covenant (Kings 19:10-14). The baby is placed on the chair of Elijah before the ceremony is performed as a sign of the covenant between generations.

This special chair, whether it is owned by the synagogue or by the family, presents another opportunity to weave a ritual Judaic textile. The weaving can be in the form of a chair cover or a pillow for the seat. Some fiber artists engineer a tailored piece of cloth for a customized fit, while others focus their attention on looser free-flowing structures. In either case the success of the piece is influenced by the chair itself and by the appropriateness of the fiber chosen. Like any weaving for a baby, an "Elijah's chair" cover or cushion must be washable.

98. *"Pillar of fire by night and pillar of clouds by day."* Ark doors by Pinky (Hermana) Shmerler, Cherry Hill, New Jersey, for Temple Oheb Shalom, Baltimore, Maryland. Fabricated in collaboration with Ascalon Studio. 1989. 8' x 5'. Plain weave with surface texture worked on the loom. Wool. These Ark doors depict the "pillar" (Exodus 13) that symbolized God's protection of the children of Israel while they were wandering in the desert. (Photograph courtesy of the artist)

Textiles for the synagogue

Handwoven items may also adorn the worship space. Such items could include a *parokhet* (Torah curtain), Torah mantles (scroll covers), and the *bimah* (lectern) cloth. It is important that these items be aesthetically pleasing, since the worshipers' attention is directed toward them for every ceremony and service that takes place in the sanctuary.

The Torah curtain and the *bimah* cloth are visible at all times; the Torah mantles are only seen when the ark is open or when the Torahs are removed. Although *shatnez* (the prohibition-against mixing fibers) must be observed, an Ark curtain is not otherwise prescribed in shape, size, or color. Its limitations come from its function and the space itself. Often the cur-

tain is divided in the center to allow easy access to the Ark doors or to the Torahs. This division can be an element in the design of the curtain. The curtain should be mounted so as to allow easy access for the person opening the curtain. The hardware and the drapability or stiffness of the handwoven cloth should be considered from the beginning of the design process.

In the Ashkenazic tradition, Torah mantles (scroll covers) are cylinders made of cloth. The bottom end is open while the top is closed by an oval made of wood or other substantial material. Usually, this oval is covered with the same material as the cylinder and has two holes cut into it for the handles of the scroll. Generally, the oval and the cylinder are sewed together for a tailored appearance. In the Sephardic tradition, the Torah mantle is an open rectangle resembling a wrap-around skirt. Most synagogues own two sets of Torah mantles. White is used for the High Holy Days, but any tasteful color or design can be used during the rest of the year.

The actual size of the cover must be individually measured, since scroll sizes vary. Extra material is needed for a Torah binder, a strip of cloth wrapped around the scroll itself to keep it from unrolling. An average-sized binder is three-inches-wide with elastic inserted inside to maintain a tight diameter. Silver buckles or other finishings are attached to the ends of the covered elasticized piece to enable the person preparing for the reading to open the rolled scroll without damaging the fragile parchment.

If you are designing appointments for a synagogue, you will want to be aware of local practices and preferences. It is always wise to consult with the rabbi before you plan a gift to a congregation.

Textiles that are permanently installed in the synagogue should be included in routine maintenance, such as vacuuming and dusting. The white Torah covers used for the High Holy Days are stored when they are not being used.

99 b. *Back view, Torah cover.* This Torah cover is fastened with Velcro® snaps; silk-covered snaps could also be used. (Photographs by Taylor Photo)

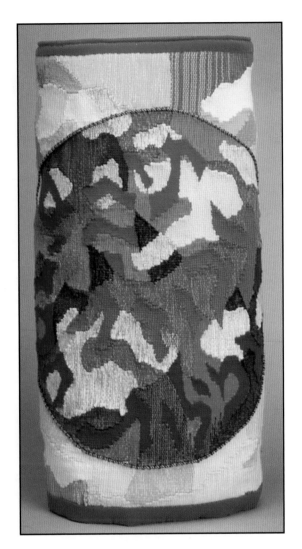

99 a. *"The World is Based on Three things…Torah, Worship, and Loving Deeds"* by Ina Golub, Mountainside, New Jersey, for Congregation Beth Am, Los Altos, California. 1995. 25″ x 12″ x 7″. Tapestry. Cotton warp; wool weft, with metallic stitchery. The theme, a phrase from the Talmud, was selected by the daily *minyan* group of Congregation Beth Am. Nature and the circle are major elements in the artist's work. Here she depicts a world floating in the universe, a world encompassing the three ideals on which Judaism is based—Torah, worship, and loving deeds.

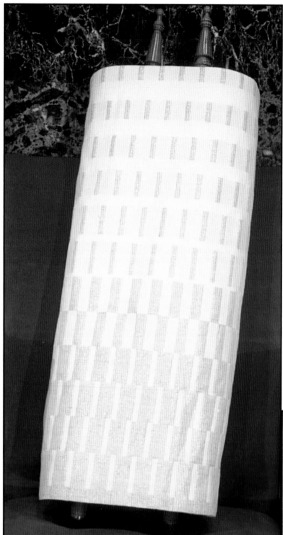

100 a. (left) *High Holy Days Torah cover* by Mary Ann Danin and Laurie Gross, Venice, California, for Washington Hebrew Congregation, Washington, D.C. 1991. 34" x 12" x 6". Double weave on an AVL Compu-dobby. 20/2 wool and gold-colored metal. White Torah covers are used to dress the Torah for the High Holy Days of Rosh Hashannah (Jewish New Year) and Yom Kippur (Day of Atonement). White symbolizes a clean start for the new year; the gold symbolizes reverence for the Torah.

100 b. (below) *Detail.* Torah covers. Washington Hebrew Congregation is a large synagogue in Washington, D. C. Their ark holds seven Torah scrolls with very elaborate silver and gold ornaments, breast plates, crowns, pointers, and handle covers, whose covers are changed to white for the High Holy Days . The challenge in designing these Torah covers was to complement the silver ornaments and yet create a design that would stand on its own. The change from dense gold to white is meant to symbolize preparation for atonement and reaching for the Divine. The gradation emphasizes the idea of change and cleansing and gives the viewer a meditative object on which to focus. (Photographs by Marvin Rand)

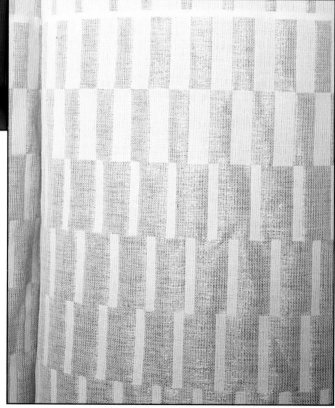

101 a. (below) *Ark curtain* by Laurie Gross and Julia Ford, Santa Barbara, California, for Congregation Beth Torah, Overland Park, Kansas. 1996-1997. 7'8" high x 11' wide. Hand-painted supplementary warp brocade. 16/1 linen ground warp, 14/4 linen supplemental warp. This Ark curtain was designed to bring warmth to a rather minimalistic worship environment. The bush design is based on the story of Moses and the burning bush in Exodus 3. The branch elements are flamelike in their design and together create an overall effect that is almost like a hand. From within the bush a white wing form emerges; upon close examination within the wing form, one can see the letter "Shin"— representing Shadai (the Lord's name)—repeatedly woven into the cloth. The "Shin" appears also in three rows at the bottom of the curtain as a reference to "holy ground" as God calls to Moses.

101 b. (right) *Detail, "Shin" design.* The first layer of the design was painted with dye onto the warp threads prior to weaving. The Hebrew letter "Shin" is integrated into the weave structure creating a second layer of the design. The final layers of design are applied to the finished surface as appliqué with detailing in embroidery and gold paint. (Photographs by Luke Jordan)

Other possibilities

Judaic weaving takes many forms that do not have specific ritual functions. The themes of Jewish festivals such as Hanukkah and Purim can be represented in textiles. The *mezuzah* – an inscribed piece of parchment contained in a case, which some believe has protective powers and others see as a mark of Jewish identity – that marks the doorpost of a Jewish home may be constructed with weaving. (See page 128.) Other objects such as a tower-shaped spice box (see page 119) or a charity *(tzedakah)* box may also be woven, although they are usually executed in metal.

Many sources can supply support and inspiration for works that represent themes in the Jewish heritage. A local weaving guild may have a group of people who are interested in studying religious traditions in weaving; Jewish and Christian weavers of ritual textiles have many common interests. Knowledgable weavers will be able to help with resources and guidelines.

Weaving books and magazines from the neighborhood library have information on Judaic traditions as does the World Wide Web. Visiting synagogues or Jewish museums will also connect the weaver with the larger tradition of Judaic weaving. In addition, Jewish agencies sometimes house a small specialty collection or know of individuals with expertise in traditional and non-traditional textiles.

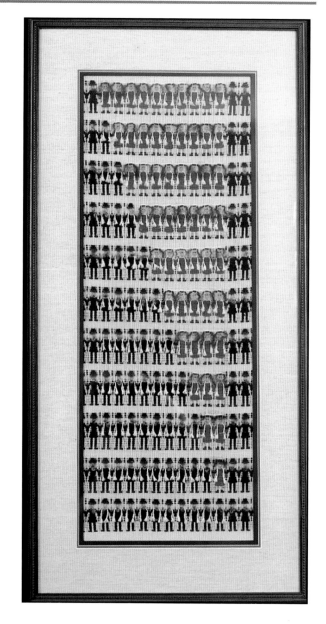

102. *"Mixed Blessing."* Wall hanging by Paula Stewart. Private collection. 1990. 40" x 12". Boundweave. Cotton with mixed fibers. "Mixed Blessing" speaks of the changing role of women in the synagogue. Each row of this wall hanging has a *minyan*—ten people—wearing prayer shawls. A *minyan* is the minimum number of Jews—ten—that must be present to enable the lawful conduct of a public Jewish service. The number of women included in the *minyan* increases by one in each row from bottom to top. (Photograph by Images by Floom)

103. (below) *"Mizrach"* by Betty Fern Edwards, Madison, Wisconsin. Private collection. 1989. 8½" x 5". Loom woven beadwork. Nylon thread and glass seed-beads. This piece incorporates the Hebrew word *mizrach* which means "east." A *mizrach* is a traditional Jewish art form which is hung on the wall in homes and synagogues to indicate the direction of Jerusalem. It is traditional for Jews to pray facing toward the site of the ancient temple. The artist was inspired by the motifs of Middle Eastern art and rugs, motifs which originate in religious traditions. (Photograph by Andrew Gillis)

104. (above) *Blue Chamsa* by Steven Medwin, Broomall, Pennsylvania. Artist's collection. 1994. 6" x 6". Weft-faced tapestry. Cotton warp, wool weft. The *chamsa* is a Middle Eastern good luck symbol designed to ward off the evil eye. The artist was inspired by *chamsas* made in filigreed metal, which in turn became the inspiration for the fine detail in this tapestry. Although a cartoon was used for the hand, the design in each diamond was improvised at the loom. (Photograph by the artist)

105. *Ark Tapestry* by Laurie dill-Kocher, Rochester, New York, for Congregation B'nai Israel, Bridgeport, Connecticut. 1992. 30' x 8'. Tapestry with lettering and olive branches created by hand-manipulated crewel. Warp is assorted fibers; weft is wool and wool/silk blend. The design for the ark tapestry is based on an illuminated page from the Cervera Bible, a work from fourteenth century Spain. It depicts Zechariah's vision of the restored Jewish state, with the viewer's focus centered on the Ten Commandments, surrounded by the peaceful vision of olive branches. A detail of this work appears on the cover of this book. (Photograph by the artist)

Chapter 8
TAPESTRIES
by Jeanette MacMillan Pruiss

106. *"Wisdom"* by Jeanette MacMillan Pruiss for the Episcopal Church of the Redeemer, Cincinnati, Ohio. 1989. 5' x 3'. Tapestry. Wool. The colors represent the experiences of life: love, birth, hate, learning, friendships, enemies, joy, sadness, and death. All these flow together and into an understanding of the universe. (Proverbs 3:13) (Photograph by the artist)

NOTE: *As this book came together, it was apparent that we had photos of many outstanding works that had been woven to adorn the walls of houses of worship. These pieces are far more than decorative work; they play an important role in inspiring the minds and the hearts of worshipers. However, they are not part of the ritual of worship as such and therefore do not fit into the preceding chapters of this book. These wall pieces have been gathered into this chapter and the next one. Many of the works illustrated in this chapter are woven in a traditional tapestry technique. Nonetheless, we do not mean to imply, either by the title of the chapter or by the grouping of the works, that wall pieces must be woven in tapestry.*

As we were making these decisions, we also saw that this essay on tapestry by Jeanette M. Pruiss was, in effect, a case study of many of the issues raised about commissions in the following chapter. We considered reversing the order of the two last chapters, but it seemed best, for a number of editorial and artistic reasons, to put the case study before the conclusions. Nevertheless, chapters 8 and 9 are intended to be read as a unit.

A WEAVER HAS many questions when a house of worship or a hospital asks about a tapestry or wall hanging.

- What does the space look like?
- What is the theme?
- What kind of design is appropriate?
- What colors will be used?
- How large should the tapestry be?
- What shape should it be?
- What fibers should be used?
- How will it be hung?
- Will it hang permanently, or in rotation with other works?

The people who are commissioning the tapestry also have questions.

- How much will it cost?
- How soon can it be completed?

These questions must be raised (if not answered) before the designing of a wall hanging begins. The examples in this chapter are drawn from my experience as the designer and

107. *"Exodus"* by Jeanette MacMillan Pruiss for the Episcopal Church of the Redeemer, Cincinnati, Ohio. 1989. 5' x 3'. Tapestry. Wool. The Israelites leave their bondage with their flocks and herds; they move toward freedom, passing valleys and hills, and walking between the waters of the Red Sea and the Promised Land. (Exodus 12:37-38.) (Photograph by the artist)

weaver of a series of tapestries for the Episcopal Church of the Redeemer in Cincinnati, Ohio. Although this project was of a larger magnitude than any of my previous commissions, it was still typical of my experience with weaving tapestries for worship spaces and serves as a basis for this chapter.

Designing for a commission

The chair of the arts committee received my name from a mutual friend for whom I had made tapestries. She asked to borrow the portfolio of commissions I had done during my 35 years as a weaver to show to other committee members.

Eventually, the committee decided they would like to meet with me. Virtually the first thing they wanted was a firm price. To determine a price, which was based on the time it would take to weave the eight tapestries, I had to know the projected size of each hanging. The committee had determined that each tapestry would be three feet by five feet and would hang vertically, like a flag, from a pole perpendicular to the wall. The tapestries would be seen from the front and the back, which meant that all ends would have to be worked in. (Tapestry is usually worked with the "wrong" side toward the artist and ends are left hanging on the surface.) Furthermore, designs could not use letters or numbers (which don't "read" backwards) and designs would have to make sense from both sides.

Since my lifestyle was not centered on weaving more than a couple of hours a day, I determined that it would take six months to weave each tapestry. In order to fulfill this order in the two years the committee wanted, I asked a good friend and excellent weaver, Evelyn Christensen, to weave half the tapestries.

When I met with the committee, I took with me samples of the yarns that would be the weft threads to compare with the stained glass windows in the space. I also took a sketchbook to make notes on the wall color, the light sources (windows and artificial light), the material of the floor covering, and the texture of the ceiling. I made observations about the furniture and about other textiles in the sanctuary such as drapes, kneeling pads, and pew cushions. I noted the color, designs, and themes of the stained glass windows. All these notes helped me refresh my memory while I was designing the tapestries.

The committee accepted my suggestion that I would use eight themes—four from the Old Testament and four from the New Testament—suggested by the minister of the church. (My approach to designing this commission is described in the second part of this chapter.) We set a date at the end of the month for a meeting with the donors, the minister, the deacons, and the committee members. At this time I presented my designs. Happily, the group decided that my designs were in keeping with their wishes:

1. Colors should lighten and brighten the gray stone interior.

2. The designs should be contemporary in feel but not completely abstract. They should show familiar objects so that worshipers could understand the theme.

3. The design should be strong and clear so as to "read" from a distance since the tapestries would hang 15 to 20 feet above the heads of the congregation.

108. (right) *"Resurrection."* Designed by Jeanette MacMillan Pruiss and woven by Evelyn Christensen for the Episcopal Church of the Redeemer, Cincinnati, Ohio. 1989. 5′ x 3′. Tapestry. Wool. An angel wing lifts the returned Jesus to heaven. The rising white and silver forms symbolize his purity and virtue. (Matthew 28:6) (Photograph by the artist)

Getting started

Start small, experiment, and learn how to solve the various problems that arise in working through a design.

Design a simple cartoon and place it behind a warp wrapped around a board. The lines of the design must be outlined with a black felt tip pen so they will show through the warp. Thread the weft yarn into one or more large-eyed needles and weave it through the warp according to the design. Pack the weft into place with the needle, the fingers, a fork, or a comb.

Weaving the tapestries

The first step in weaving a tapestry is to choose the warp and weft threads, which will determine the sett and the amount of yarn that will be required. The warp for this project was 8/3 Swedish rug linen, sett 36 inches wide at ten e.p.i. The warp was ten yards long, which allowed for four tapestries each five feet long—plus hems, fringe, and retying after each one.

At the beginning of each tapestry, I put a row of twining across the warp to space the warp threads evenly, and followed it with a few rows of plain weave to give a base to the tapestry. (The exact number of rows should vary according to whether the tapestry will be fringed or finished with a hem or a heading.) The plain weave could be the warp thread or a softer material that would pack in better.

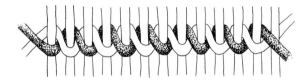

Twining

My loom is a vertical tapestry loom; I use a hand beater. The cartoon, which I draw with a felt tip marker on artist's canvas rather than paper, sits behind the warp threads as a guide for weaving. The canvas is long enough to allow the cartoon to be pinned to the hem at the bottom of the tapestry and draped over a cord which runs from one side of the top of loom to the other. Thus the entire design is visible behind the warp threads. The canvas cartoon should be placed as close to the warp threads as possible to avoid distortion in the finished weaving.

Many brands of weft threads are available; the ones used for the eight tapestries were Paternayan needlepoint yarns because of the wide range of colors. In addition, strands were

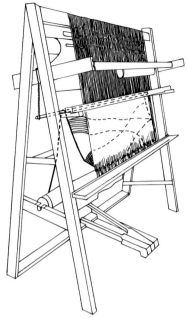

In this drawing of a vertical tapestry loom, the cartoon is represented by the dotted lines behind the warp. The cartoon drapes over a stick that hangs from the superstructure of the loom. The cartoon is pinned behind the tapestry and rolls onto the beam with it.

separated and recombined to blend new colors. I also used Borgs "Lundagarn," a fine wool from Sweden that Swedish weavers use for tapestry weaving. These yarns were wound into butterflies as needed.

The balance between the size of the weft and the sett of the warp is crucial in tapestry weaving. If the weft is too fine relative to the warp, the threads will pack and build up, creating a loose structure. On the other hand, a weft that is too thick or stiff will not pack well and will leave the warp showing. In some fabrics it is desirable to have the warp showing, but in traditional tapestry it is not. A 3/2 cotton warp sett at ten e.p.i. will work well when the weft is two or three strands of Paternayan yarn. This combination will give a good firm structure, in which the weft covers the warp completely. A sample to check warp, weft, and sett can be made on a piece of foam core by wrapping the warp around the board for several inches and then weaving the weft yarn with a needle.

Tapestry techniques are a matter of personal preference. Different techniques work for different types of designs. For example, the technique called vertical slit (where bobbins meet and separate in opposite directions) is useful for shading, while a slit tapestry technique (where bobbins do not share a warp thread as they turn) will give a sharp line of color change. Diagonal slit tapestry (where the slit caused by meeting bobbins is on an angle) is useful for building shapes. Anyone attempting to weave a tapestry should have a thorough knowledge of a number of techniques.

SOME TAPESTRY TECHNIQUES

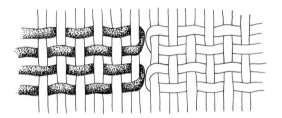

A slit tapestry will give sharp changes of color.

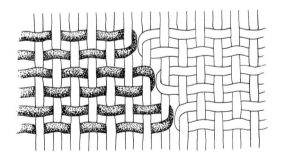

A diagonal slit is useful for building shapes.

109. *"The Coming of the Holy Spirit"* by Jeanette MacMillan Pruiss for the Episcopal Church of the Redeemer, Cincinnati, Ohio. 1989. x5′ x 3′. Tapestry. Wool. The strong winds overhead represent the Holy Spirit descending to the multitudes and the flames that came from them as they spoke in tongues after receiving the Holy Spirit. (Acts 2:2–3.) (Photograph by the artist)

DESIGNING A TAPESTRY

When I studied with the Finnish tapestry weaver, Eva Antilla, she had us draw a simple line design and enlarge and change it through sixteen variations. I asked her, "What if variation nine is better than number sixteen?" Her answer was "Oh, no! Never! You keep improving until you know it is the best!"

The first sketches for "Abba," and there were many, attempted to show a human face for "Father" and a pouch or enclosure for the protection of the humans.

While I am not sure that the last idea is always the best idea, my method of designing tapestries is based on this way of refining and abstracting from a realistic design. While I am paying attention to line, shape, tone, and texture—and my designs can be evaluated according to the rules of balance, emphasis, proportion, unity, and rhythm—I am ultimately looking for a design that satisfies me.

I take my inspiration from many sources. I keep in my "art morgue" a box full of papers, magazine pages, scraps, and cards. Each is a picture, a drawing, a photo, or a sketch that could be the inspiration for a design. Some of these I have used and some I may never use, but they are there, just waiting for the right theme to come along.

After I had received the eight suggested themes for the tapestries—four from the Old Testament and four from the New—I pulled out this box. In going through the collection, I asked myself if the lines or parts of designs could be used to represent one of the themes. If my answer was "yes" or even "maybe," I put the design aside to look at again. I can't remember which designs started the building process, but I remember it as an exciting time; creativity lifts the spirit as possibilities rush forward.

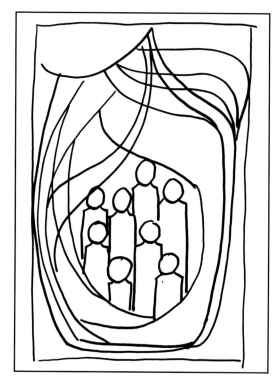

Here is a further thought: expressing "Father" as a dynamic arc with enclosing lines descending from the arc to the pouch protecting the humans.

Usually the first lines were simple suggestions of the theme; more complex lines were added until I had a complete design. Eventually I added color to produce the final product. Since these hangings were designed to be seen from 15 to 20 feet below, the colors needed to be strong and the designs simple, so the message could be "read" by the viewers. I stayed with a limited number of colors so that the eight tapestries would work together visually.

110. *"Abba."* Designed by Jeanette MacMillan Pruiss and woven by Evelyn Christensen for the Episcopal Church of the Redeemer, Cincinnati, Ohio. 1989. 5' x 3'. Tapestry. Wool. The arms of the Father enfold all the races of the world as they cry "Abba, Father" and acknowledge his omnipotence. (Romans 8:15) (Photograph by the artist)

Enlarging the design

One way to transfer a design to a canvas is to copy it on a copier and make a grid across the copy. Make a grid with the same number, but larger, blocks on a 3' x 5' cartoon canvas. Reproduce the lines from the design block by block—at a larger scale—onto the canvas. Use a black felt tip marker to draw the design; fill in the spaces with colored markers.

Another way to enlarge a design is to photocopy the design onto a transparency and project the transparency onto the fabric that will be the cartoon.

Hanging a tapestry

Hanging a tapestry is part of the presentation. Since the eight tapestries for the Church of the Redeemer were designed to hang from rods that extended from the wall, I needed some sort of casing loop, or sleeve, through which the rod would pass.

At the top of the weaving, I wove several rows of plain weave as I had at the beginning of the weaving and made a row of twining across the width. I applied white glue to the twining to keep it from slipping when the tapestry was cut from the loom. Then I cut the warp (leaving an allowance of several inches), unrolled the tapestry, and glued the twining at the beginning edge. (The glue must be allowed to dry before the bouts of warp on the cloth beam rod are cut.)

I had designed the hangings to have black loops at the top and a black casing at the bottom. When we could not find commercial cloth that was acceptable, we decided to weave all the black bands as well. We ran a flag pole through the loops and placed a small dowel in the bottom casing to maintain a straight edge without a drape. The hardware for the wall attachments came from a commercial flag store.

Another way to finish a tapestry is to hem the ends: simply weave enough plain weave on each end for a hem. Another finish is to make a fringe from the extra warp at one or both ends; it is possible to attach supplementary warp fringe if the fringe is not attractive. Fringe can be braided, twisted, or allowed to hang free. If a rigid look is preferred to a natural drape, the tapestry can be mounted on wood, though plywood and wood with high acid emissions should be avoided. If the hanging is not too large, it can be stapled on stretcher strips; the back may be covered with acid-free craft paper for a neater finish.

111. *"Incarnation."* Designed by Jeanette MacMillan Pruiss and woven by Evelyn Christensen for the Episcopal Church of the Redeemer, Cincinnati, Ohio. 1989. 5' x 3'. Tapestry. Wool. Mother and child are enfolded in the arms of the Almighty. The yellow represents the Holy Spirit. (Luke 2:7) (Photograph by the artist)

Care of a tapestry

The committee members asked how to care for the tapestries after they were installed. I advised them to remove them from the poles each year, vacuum them on both sides, and spray with a moth repellent before rehanging.

A hanging system that makes it easy to take the tapestry down and put it back up will make it easier to care for it properly.

An extended discussion of "Hanging Methods that Work and Last" can be found in issue 98 (spring 1994) of *Shuttle Spindle & Dyepot.*

Weaving for hospitals

Weaving for hospital chapels or other non-denominational settings has special requirements. Frequently, the design must be inspirational but not carry the iconography of any specific religious group. The artists whose work is illustrated on the following pages have drawn their imagery from various sources. In one case an artist studied the literature of an ethnic group within whose neighborhood the hospital stood.

Certain themes such as peace, healing, strength, love, care, and compassion are popular in these settings. In addition, themes involving care for the earth seem to be evocative. It is not unusual for such works to be memorial gifts given in gratitude for care given to a family member. Such memorials can be marked by a plaque or an embroidered tag. (See page 67.)

Likewise, nursing homes, colleges, and private schools may request woven works for their chapels. For these settings, it is important for the artist to attend worship and become familiar with local practices and concerns.

112. *"Healing Flight"* by Ulrika Leander, Oak Ridge, Tennessee, for St. Michael's Hospital, Texarkana, Texas. 1994. 12′ x 5′. Tapestry. Cotton warp, wool weft. This tapestry hangs in an area dominated by windows; the artist wanted to create a feeling of open sky in the tapestry. By building the color from almost black up to sky tones using different geometric shapes, she was able to create the effect of another window. (Photograph by J. W. Nave)

113. *Chancel tapestry* by Barbara Berg, Decorah, Iowa, for Mayo Clinic, Rochester, Minnesota. 1994. 6' x 4'. Theo Moorman technique. Wool, rayon, cotton. This tapestry takes its inspiration from Psalm 121, "I lift up my eyes to the hills…" It was designed for a psychiatric care facility, so its theme had to be non-denominational. (Photograph by the Mayo Clinic)

114 a, b. *The Seasons: Winter, Summer* (above)*; Spring, Fall* (right) by Shirley Herrick, Fridley, Minnesota, for Fairview Riverside Hospital, Minneapolis. 1995-1996. Four pieces, each 106" x 39". Plain weave, rosepath, twill. Wool. This hospital is in an ethnic neighborhood. Native Americans see the eagle as the power of the Great Spirit. The deer represents gentleness, love, and compassion. The buffalo signals a time of abundance and plenty. Water is a primary life source. It nourishes the meadows and the valleys which are symbols of new life, new fertility, and developing creativity. (Photographs by Peter Lee)

115. *Banner* by Norman Frankland, Twin Bridges, Montana. Property of the Church of the Valley, Twin Bridges. 1996. 6' x 4'. Weft-faced tapestry. Wool. The artist designed this piece to be placed behind the tabernacle in a Catholic church. When the recipient found the banner to be "liturgically incorrect," the artist gave it to the Church of the Valley. The primary colors employed represent the basic foundation of the Christian faith.
(Photograph by Carl Basner)

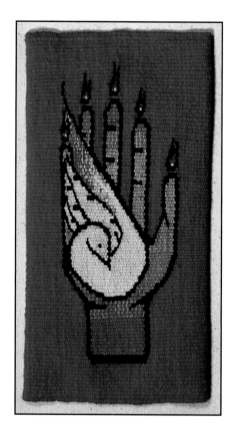

116. *"Pentecost Peace"* by Constance Hunt, San Francisco, California. Private collection. 10½"x 5½". Tapestry. Wool with cotton warp. With the spirit-dove becoming a part of the upraised hand, empowerment takes form and flows forth from the flaming fingertips to create, work, and be in the world.
(Photograph by Gary Hunt)

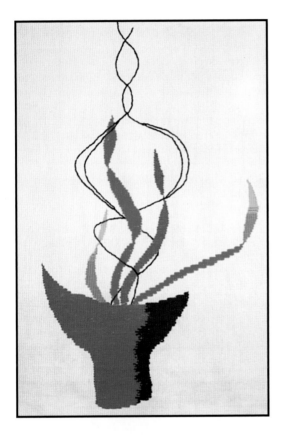

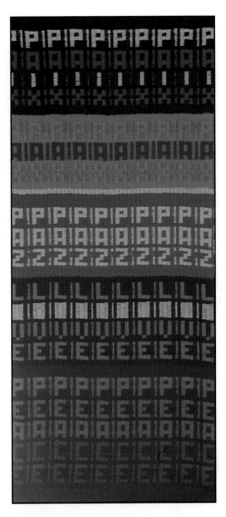

117. *"Flaming Chalice"* by Barbara Meyers, Fremont, California, for Mission Peak Unitarian Universalist Congregation, Fremont. 1994. 48" x 36". Theo Moorman technique. Wool. The flaming chalice was originally a symbol representing the martyrdom of the fifteenth century Bohemian heretic, Jan Hus, who was burned at the stake for letting all congregants, not just priests, drink from the communion chalice. This symbol was widely adopted by Unitarian Universalists after World War II. This piece was designed as a worship centerpiece for a newly formed church. (Photograph by Walter J. Arrufat)

118. *Peace Banner* by Zenaide Reiss, Milford, New Jersey, for Atlanta Friends Meeting, Atlanta, Georgia. 1980. 47" x 20". Boundweave. Linen warp, wool weft. This is a bright and joyous expression of the Quaker concepts of peace and love. The use of several languages was a an attempt to reinforce the universality of these concepts. (Photograph by Fred Gonnerman)

119 a. (left) *"Burst of Life"* Christmas/Easter banner designed by Richard R. Caemmerer, Jr., woven by Suzanne Halvorson, and appliquéed by Patsy Zawistoski for Imanuel Lutheran Church, New York City. 1996. 12' x 42". Plain weave. Rayon chenille. This is one of a set of five seasonal banners for this church by this collaborative team. Caemmerer lives in Leavenworth, Washington; Halvorson, in Bloomington, Indiana; and Zawistoski, in Elletsville, Indiana. This particular design was inspired by "The burst of life from the Eternal Circle which recalls the new life in the manger and the resurrected life in the tomb." The banners are designed to complement the stained glass at Imanuel, which is also by Caemmerer. (Photographs by Jens Mortensen)

119 b. (below) *Detail* of "Burst of Life." This design required fifty-seven yards of handwoven chenille in 48 colors. Rayon chenille has a glasslike reflective quality unlike any other handwoven fabric. Metallic threads were combined with some colors to enhance the luster of the fabric. Black wool outlines the jewel colors to create a stained glass effect. The woven fabric was backed with cotton/poly before it was appliquéed.

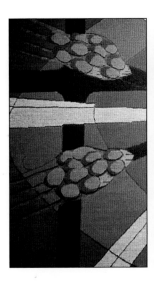

120. "Communing with Christ" by Kaino Leethem, Boring, Oregon, for St. Paul of Damascus Lutheran Church, Boring. 1995. Three pieces. Center 72" high; sides 60" high. All 36" across. Plain weave with transparency. Linen. This hanging combines the Chi and Rho (symbols for Christ) with the elements of communion, grapes and wheat. The colors were selected to go with colors existing in the church—purple floor and red seat covers. The design was enlarged with an overhead projector to actual size, from which the paper cartoon was made. Although this work was a gift to the artist's church, she consulted with many people in the church before she began to weave it. (Photograph by Richard Duncan)

121. (right) *Matka Boska: The Mother of God"* by Danita Ostasiewski McDonald, Greensboro, North Carolina. Artist's collection. 1995. 10" x 8". Double weave pick-up. Cotton embroidery thread. This piece was inspired by all the icons the artist has lived with since childhood. It combines faith and culture, warmth and home. The artist found it a prayerful experience to chart and then weave this "meditation" on an icon. One problem was to figure out how to include many rich, warm colors while working in only two layers. The artist solved the problem by using one variegated layer of traditional icon colors and another layer of deep blue. (Photograph by John Skau)

122 a. *"Grace be to you and peace"* by Ulrika Leander, Oak Ridge, Tennessee, for Grace Lutheran Church, Oak Ridge. 1987. 168" x 126". Tapestry. Warp is 12/6 cotton; weft is wool. Working with a commission usually imposes certain limitations. This sanctuary is almost as wide as it is deep and the immediate problem was to make the tapestry appear much wider than its actual size. A broader look was achieved by separating the four central towers to reveal the background with its horizontal lines, and to interrupt the continuity of the flowing gold lines.

122 b. (right) The sanctuary had green carpeting throughout; to counterbalance the carpet, red was chosen as the principal color for the tapestry. The white spaces on either side were deliberately left empty to focus attention on the harmonious working of altar, cross, and tapestry. Ninety different blends of colors were used in the tapestry. (Photographs by J.W. Nave)

Chapter 9
COMMISSIONS
by Lucy Brusic

123. *Spice Container I* by Ina Golub, Mountainside, New Jersey. In the permanent collection of the Jewish Museum, New York, New York. 1995. 7" x 2½" x 2½". Beadwork. Glass beads, wire. The artist intended this piece to reflect Jewish tradition while making a contemporary statement. She was inspired by sculptural ceremonial objects in the Israel Museum in Jerusalem. She wove this piece in two strips on a bead loom using a warp of brass wire and weft of Japanese beads on Kevlar thread. The strips were manipulated to form the architectural tower typical of European spice containers. (Photograph by Taylor Studio)

NOT MANY artists have the opportunity for their work to function in a religious communal environment. This is a privilege which does not allow for personal idiosyncrasies, but carries a heavy responsibility. There is an audience out there which needs to respond with sympathy to an art which awakens religious feelings. This gives the artist the freedom to search, invent, and to innovate. This implies much thought, knowledge, and an understanding for the needs, traditions, and spirit of the community.

Avram Kampf, Ein Hod, Israel, August 1995, in *Ina Golub: The Work of the Weaver in Colors* (New York: Yeshiva University Museum, 1996).

WEAVERS WHO are commissioned to produce work for Jewish or Christian worship communities produce different objects with different design considerations according to the customs of the religious tradition for which they are weaving. A weaver working for a synagogue will have to observe the rules of the Judaic textile tradition, and a weaver working for a church will have to observe the protocols of the Christian textile tradition. These historical constraints sometimes make it seem as though Christian and Jewish weavers are doing different things, as the division of chapters in this book tends to suggest.

Nevertheless, enough common ground exists between the two endeavors to create a general picture of what is involved in being a professional liturgical weaver. This chapter attempts to set forth that common ground by drawing upon the experiences of Marjorie Ford, Ina Golub, Marc Hamel, Joyce Harter, Edward LeSage, Steve Medwin, and Joyce Rettstadt.

As Avram Kampf's remarks suggest, being a commissioned weaver of items for churches and synagogues is a serious commitment of time and faith. It can be a rewarding, but also a frustrating, way to express commitment and artistic vision. It presupposes that the artist has a thorough grounding in and respect for the religious tradition in which she or he is working. It also presupposes that the artist is a skilled professional in his or her craft. At a hands-on level, it assumes that the artist-as-weaver has acquired the skill to do high quality weaving efficiently.

Dr. Kampf's remarks also emphasize that religious artists have a responsibility—beyond their own artistic vision—to the congregation and to the tradition. On the one hand, the artist must respond to the context—the needs and the proclivities—of the community. At the same time the artist should respect both the sacred tradition and his or her own artistic integrity. At times, the artist may need the insight to turn down a commission if it appears that the client does not understand the artist's creative or liturgical style.

Getting started

An artist needs a portfolio—a photographic record of work—to enter the field. One can begin a portfolio with photographs of secular pieces that illustrate the artist's style. The weaver can include ritual pieces—such as Torah covers or paraments—which have been made as samples or entered in shows or exhibits. (In other words, an artist does not have to have professionally commissioned work to create a portfolio.)

Some, but not all, weavers suggested making clergy stoles or tallitot for gifts and then including pictures of those works in a portfolio. Although all the artists respected the tradition of personal gifts of hand work to reli-

124. *Wall hangings* by Bill Rafnel, Vista, California, for the First Church of Religious Science, Fallbrook, California. 1987. Three panels, each 6' x 4'. False damask on a AVL Compu-dobby loom. Linen. A horizontal gold line aligns all three pieces, with the colors moving from dark to light through the center piece. The center panel was designed to hang lower to symbolize the heights and depths of human life. The artist used two warps for this work: one for the side panels and another for the center one. These panels are attached by Velcro® to boards at the top and weighted with rods at the bottom. (Photograph by Corel Blanco)

gious institutions and some felt that an outright gift to a church or a synagogue was a good way to get started, others say that for a professional artist to give away work undermines the standards of the field.

However the artist amasses enough work to create a portfolio, the pieces should be photographed professionally. Professional photography sends the message that the artist is serious about being respected as a professional. One weaver said that she felt she had increased her income by at least twice as much as she had paid for quality photography over the years.

A portfolio will also include a resumé with a list of commissions and the names of one or two persons who can be asked for recommendations. Churches, synagogues, and individuals who are considering commissions want assurance that their project will be finished on time and within budget. Finished work—and word of mouth—will always be the best advertisement an artist can have.

Photographs can also be used to create a slide presentation to show to church or synagogue groups. Since many congregations have little education in religious art, such talks may have a strong educational message. Nevertheless, they are an excellent form of self-promotion.

Another way to advertise is to have a well-designed brochure to send to congregations working with new buildings, or approaching an anniversary. A brochure might contain one or two excellent photos, some kind of a resumé, and an address or other contact information. Targeted mailings are fruitful; mass mailings are not. In the Christian church, the best time to send brochures is in September or in late spring (after Easter); within Judaism, after the High Holy Days or after Passover.

A write-up in a local paper or religious publication is also good advertising; don't hesitate to send press releases about installations, speeches, or awards. Speaking or displaying work at religious gatherings is another way to contact potential customers. Some weavers find it profitable to advertise in religious publications; others feel that such advertising is a waste of money.

125. *"All One in Christ Jesus"* by Marjorie Ford for Saint Paul Lutheran Church, St. Paul, Minnesota. 1988. 4'6" high x 4'3" wide x 4" deep. Balanced plain weave using tapestry joins and painted warp. Wool, silk, metallic. This piece was created for the fellowship area of a congregation that emphasizes inclusiveness. In the sanctuary of the building, the chancel wall carries a mural showing the diversity of people coming to worship. This piece conveys the obverse of that image: it stresses the unity of people within worship. The warp was painted with textile pigments before weaving to emphasize the movement from the dark chaotic outer areas to the center of light. Traditional tapestry dovetail joins highlight the edges of the color areas. The woven pieces are stretched on light metal frames and mounted at various distances from the wall. (Photograph by the artist)

Working with clients

STEP 1. THE APPROACH

Most artists send a brochure and a cost sheet in response to any inquiry. Several find it useful to follow up an initial inquiry with a note or letter after six weeks and then again in six months. Generally, it is clear at the end of six weeks whether a client is interested or not, although it sometimes takes two to three years for a commission to be finalized.

Some weavers will refer potential clients to slide libraries or other sites to see examples of the type of work under consideration. In general, this strategy is suggested in the hope that, by the time the first interview (see below) takes place, the committee will have decided that they want to work with a specific artist whose style and approach they like. For obvious reasons dealing with cost, weavers sometimes find it difficult to compete successfully with artists working in other media and don't wish to put themselves into an open competition with them.

Many artists do not like to enter design competitions unless they are paid at least a nominal fee for their designs. For the experience of one artist, see the caption on page 127.

STEP 2. THE FIRST INTERVIEW

When clients express further interest—especially if they have expressed exclusive interest—the follow-up is usually a meeting with a committee to show slides and samples. (One weaver developed a slide show that she could mail so that congregations at a distance could work through the decision process without a site visit.) The committee may include members of the congregation, the rabbi or pastor, an architect, and a liturgical design consultant.

Whether or not a donor should be invited to this meeting is complicated. Most weavers felt that a pictorial portfolio was a useful tool in inspiring potential donors to contribute art work to a church or synagogue. On the other hand, all the weavers felt that having the donor at the first interview was sometimes a problem since the design decisions for a congregation usually require a broad—rather than an individual—perspective. A middle-of-the-road approach may be to let the committee decide what the project will be and then solicit donors for various parts of it. Of course, the donors should be recognized publicly and on the individual pieces. (See page 67).

All of the weavers compared this first meeting with an educational talk, since in many cases clients or committees do not know exactly what it is that they want to purchase, nor are they aware of all the options that are open to them. Furthermore, members of the committee may have little or no background in art, especially art for use in worship and worship spaces. The weaver who wishes to pursue commissions in liturgical art should be thoroughly grounded in the history and use of art in worship and be able to present this information in a friendly, but professional, manner.

The artist can facilitate both the educational and the decision-making process by asking such questions as

Who is this piece for? The clergy? A small group? The religious school? The congregation?

Is it to be used in the liturgy?
If so, then the weaver-as-educator should explain the role of the prospective piece and make the point that anything used in the service of worship should be subordinate to the worship experience rather than call attention to itself. In some cases, the object—vestments or a tallit—is an integral part of the liturgy and is subject to certain strictures. In other cases, an object, such as a wall hanging, may be a more independent expression of faith.

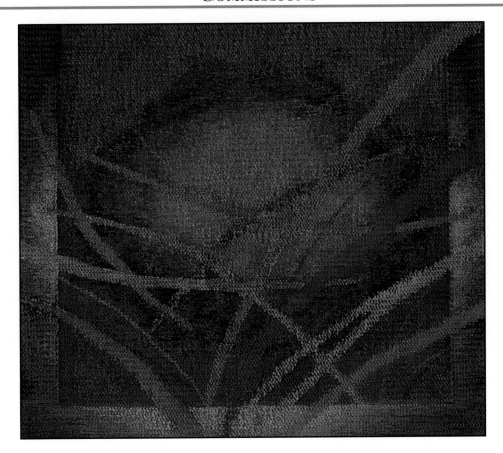

126 a. *"Reflection"* Lenten parament by Betty Vera, New York, New York, for Palisades Presbyterian Church, Palisades, New York. 1995. 24" x 25". Painted warp tapestry on broken twill. 6/2 pima cotton warp; other cottons in weft. The challenge in weaving "Reflection" was to make the central purple field rich and deep but not too dark, so that the parament would be visible throughout the church. In addition, the lighting in the church is dim and varied. The paraments must be visible on overcast days as well as sunny ones. They are also used during candlelight services. All the hues in these paraments evoke the brilliance, clarity, and purity of stained glass. (Photograph by the artist)

126 b. (right) *Pulpit with parament.* This church is long and narrow; the pulpit is the focal point. When the sanctuary was renovated, a set of six paraments was commissioned for the pulpit. The paraments are the same size (dictated by the size of the pulpit) and have similar borders and design elements. The artist first rendered the designs in watercolor mockups. She wove the paraments on one long warp, which she split into layers for painting so that the colors would be optical mixtures of many dots of color. She painted and wove each parament before proceeding to the next one. (Photograph by Adam Reich)

If the piece is to be used by the whole congregation, what is the attitude of the congregation about visual representation in art?

Congregational members may be suspicious of abstract art because it is open to a range of interpretations. Or they may not know what symbols they might use. (They may not even understand all of the symbols presently in the sanctuary; the artist can perform a very valuable function by educating committees about symbols.) An artist who is thoroughly grounded in liturgical art and practice can often see new and appropriate ideas that will enlarge the way a congregation looks at art.

What is the attitude of the congregation about purchasing art work in general?

Sometimes congregations do not understand that religious art is, historically and presently, more than a decorative add-on. They may even be hostile to the idea that money that could be spent on practical things will be spent on artwork. The response of committee members to the artist's slides at this initial meeting can be useful clues in deciding how to frame a proposal.

Where will the art be placed? Is it a permanent installation or will it be stored for some of the year?

If possible, at this first meeting, the weaver should also look at the physical surroundings, especially at the architectural style of the space and the colors already present in it, such as rugs and cushions. It is important to view the colors under as many types of light as possible, since colors are perceived differently in daylight, artificial light, or candle light. Colors will be changed by light coming through stained glass. A knowledge of what may happen to the acoustics in a sanctuary is also helpful to the artist. Be clear about how the work will be installed. If it is not a permanent installation, then accommodation to existing storage facilities should be included in the design. It is appropriate to take both measurements and photos at this first meeting if it seems likely that a proposal will be requested.

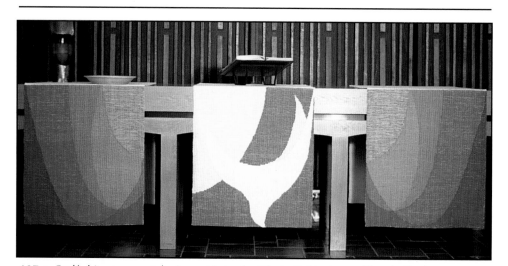

127 a. *Red/white paraments* by Joyce Harter for Gloria Dei Lutheran Church, Rochester, Minnesota. 1984. Three panels. Each panel is 35" x 30". Theo Moorman technique. Rayon and linen. This free-standing altar suggested a design for a parament that could be used for two different seasons of the church year. Since the Moorman technique allows a warp to be completely covered with another color of yarn, it was possible to create red and white combination paraments. The red yarns and symbols for the festival of Pentecost are illustrated.

What if it is clear that the amount of money the committee has to spend will not buy what they want?

It is sometimes useful to present another possibility along the lines of "This is what you can do for the amount that you have in mind. It won't be same, but it can be done."

STEP 3. THE PROPOSAL

After the initial meeting, the next step is for the artist to create a written proposal describing
- *the type of piece*
- *what size it will be*
- *how it will be hung*
- *how much it will cost*
- *and when   1) a sample and a drawing, and*
  2) the finished piece
  will be delivered.

Some weavers specified at this time whether they would take a pictorial or an abstract approach to a project. Most weavers found that production time—from first contact to finished product—was nine to fifteen months.

STEP 4. THE DESIGN PRESENTATION

Further interest on the part of the congregation will require a design presentation. In general, a design presentation includes a site drawing, a design drawing, a woven sample, and a sample of all the yarn colors that will be used. A model may be used for three-dimensional pieces.

The question of money arises at this point; weavers should not be expected to provide sketches without being paid for them. Ten or twenty percent of the finished cost (to be applied to the total cost) is the recommended amount to ask for when drawings are submitted. One artist asks a flat fee of $500 for sketches.

The weavers were divided as to how many ideas they would submit in this presentation. One weaver said she would submit only one design. Another said she would present only one design if she was absolutely sure, otherwise she would present several rough (but no complete) designs. Another said that he would never go in with only one proposal. Rather he would present five different designs, or one or

127 b. *Red/White paraments* by Joyce Harter, showing reverse, Christmas and Easter side, side of paraments in the preceding plate (127 a). This parament is one of three combination sets. The others are a blue-purple set for Advent and Lent and a green set with two different themes for the long season of Pentecost. The panels that cross the table are plain weave. These combination paraments eased expense and storage problems for this congregation. (Photographs by Neal Olson)

two with options and decisions of placement or scale, in order to give the committee a feeling of ownership. A flaw in this arrangement is that it can take a committee a very long time to make a decision between even two proposals. No artist had found an effective way to speed up a committee's decision, although several said that the deadlines imposed by a celebration or a religious holiday were often a blessing in disguise.

STEP 5. REVISIONS

The drawing is revised if necessary. One artist limits the number of revisions to one and sets a time limit (two to three weeks) during which revisions can be made.

STEP 6. THE CONTRACT

A production agreement is signed which specifies (for example) that 50% of the cost will be paid at the time of signing the contract. Such an amount is necessary to cover the purchase of materials. The contract also specifies when the rest of the money will be paid. Contracts should spell out in as much detail as possible exactly what will be done and when; in some cases it may be necessary to say that work cannot continue unless payment is forthcoming. A contract should also describe who will be responsible for delivery and installation of the work and at what cost. It is also appropriate to ask for agreement on the "rights of the artist in the piece"; that is, what will happen to the piece if it is damaged or moved to another location. Will the artist be paid to come and rehang it? This consideration is particularly crucial with large architectural pieces. It may also be wise to limit the artist's responsibility if the piece is improperly stored or cleaned.

A contract may also specify that the artist will be responsible for any flaws that appear in the work within the first year. One weaver says that she guarantees the yarns in so far as they are guaranteed to her by the manufacturer.

How to price

Different artists offered different formulas. The most exact, worked out by an accountant, was as follows: Take the materials cost and the hourly cost of the labor and add them together. Multiply the resulting sum by 20% to account for overhead. Add these two figures (materials and labor + 20% of materials and labor) together and multiply the resulting number by 10% to allow for profit. Add the 10% to the first figure to determine cost.

Thus:

Materials + labor+20% [materials+ labor]=A (costs)

A x10%=B (profit)

A+B= cost+ profit (the amount to ask from a client)

A similar but slightly more detailed formula can be found in *Weaving Profits*, by James Dillehay or similar books on marketing crafts. Such books usually contain sample contracts and other useful information for fabric artists.

Other artists have simpler formulas, based on their experience. One simply asks for a set amount, based upon years of very precise records, per square foot of vertical drop. Another takes the cost of materials and multiplies by four. Other artists have looked at prices charged by catalog houses and have priced accordingly.

All the artists found that they could charge higher prices as their reputations increased and their work acquired some prestige value. One way to add value to work is to have a thoroughly professional design presentation. Good selling techniques will enhance the artist's reputation and increase the prices she or he can command.

Unless the price being asked is extraordinarily high, there is no reason to have to explain to a client how the artist arrived at a price.

Don't quit the day job

It is very difficult to make a living exclusively from weaving for churches and synagogues. Although art pieces command high prices, handweaving is not always thought of as art and people find it hard to accept the cost of the labor to produce it. The consensus is that artists should price their time at a certain level and not undersell themselves just to get a commission.

However, there are ways to reduce costs. One suggestion was not to charge for administrative time at the beginning. Another recommendation was to look at ways to become more efficient. Not only did this suggestion involve long warps and fly shuttles, but it also included the following ideas:

- Have the delivery person come to your house.

- Employ an accountant or a legal advisor.

- Find student apprentices to thread looms or weave for you. Students are preferred over experienced weavers.

- Keep several projects going. Although this will increase the administrative load, it will mean that you can keep an apprentice busy more productively. Even if you have to buy more looms, your output will increase.

- Employ others to do things you cannot do quickly—a seamstress to do finishing or an artist to do cartoons. Figure these costs into your overhead.

- Balance creativity and craft; clients do not want to pay for experiments.

- Remember that you will become more efficient as you gain experience.

128. Parament for Christmas and Easter by Marjorie Ford for Roseville Lutheran Church, Roseville, Minnesota. 1988. 8' wide x 3' high x 6" deep. Multi-layer plain weave with supplementary weft. Wool and metallic. This congregation undertook a mini-design competition for a new white parament. They sent out specifications to artists whose work might be appropriate for a contemporary space. Interested artists submitted slides. The committee chose several artists for on-site interviews. This process gave the artists a clear understanding of the client's needs and desires. This, the winning, piece was woven in three layers, with a fourth strip woven separately and stitched on in the lowest position. The parament is positioned on the altar by attaching it with Velcro® to a white fabric which crosses the altar top and holds counterweights on the back side. During seasons when the parament does not hang on the altar, it can be exhibited in the library. The change of venue is accomplished by removing the parament from the white fabric and attaching it to a wood mounting piece on the wall. (Photograph by the artist)

Steve Medwin's experience

Steve Medwin has had a different experience. During a year in Israel, while his wife was studying to be a rabbi, Steve, an engineer, studied weaving full time. He wove many tapestries, but discovered that people would not buy them. Toward the end of his year, he came to the idea of combining weaving with the "most popular piece of Judaica sold—the mezuzah. These were functional in a religious sense; they were small so they could be produced quickly; and they sold."

At first his price was based on how many hours went into each piece and how much he wanted to make per hour, plus the cost of materials. When he took an order from a wholesaler, he found he had to improve his weaving and increase his efficiency to meet the demand, because the distributor wanted a larger discount than simple wholesale. At the same time, Steve found that the market for mezuzahs would bear almost twice the price he had been charging at craft fairs. (His mezuzahs sell for the same price whether they are sold through a distributor or at a craft fair.) The profit margin of producing for a wholesale market is about the same as producing for a craft fair, because much of the profit at a craft fair is eaten up by selling costs and the fact that you are weaving on speculation.

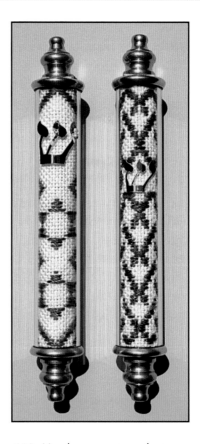

129. *Handwoven mezuzah cases*: Star of David and Endless Knot by Steven Medwin, Broomall, Pennsylvania. First produced in 1995. 4" x 1¾" before being put into tube. Inlay on plain weave ground. Variegated cotton on cotton background. A mezuzah is a prayer found inside a decorative case that is placed on the doorposts of Jewish homes. Developing a handwoven mezuzah case was a combination of engineering, designing, and weaving. The Star of David is the most widely recognized symbol of Judaism so it was a logical choice. The endless knot design represents the continuity of life. When the artist wove this design for the first time, he noticed a Star of David appearing in the middle—without being planned. (Photograph by the artist)

Pitfall

The greatest pitfall in the field of commission weaving for churches and synagogues is accepting too much work and not being able to complete it on time. It is very important to meet deadlines, as religious groups often have specific events such as anniversaries or holy days on which they wish to dedicate new items for the worship space. Always allow extra time; an organization would far rather hear that a piece is done early than that it will not be done in time.

What churches and synagogues can do to make sure they have a good relationship with artists

- Select an artist with whom you are comfortable.

- Treat the artist as a professional consultant; he or she has many years of training and experience.

- Respect the artist's business sense by honoring the contract drawn up by the artist, just as you would a contract for any professional.

- Once a contract is signed, appoint one member of the committee as the contact person for day-to-day questions as they arise.

- Pay the artist's bills on time. An artist cannot sustain a creative vision if she or he must beg for payment.

- Be willing to pay a fair price for the artist's labor. Do not expect that a self-employed artist, even one who is a member of your church or synagogue, will be able to afford to give away his or her materials or labor.

- Budget for the purchase of art. Create an environment in which art does not have to compete for funding.

- Revive the study of religious art history at every level—from kindergarten to adult education.

- Collect art books for the library. Have seminars on art.

- Recognize the contributions of artists in the worship environment.

- Seek out artists to supply handcrafted objects for use in the worship environment rather than relying on catalog goods.

- Encourage donors to contribute to the purchase of art works for the worship setting.

- Appoint visually sensitive people to liturgical arts selection committees.

- If you decide to have a design competition, draw up a description of the project, invite artists to compete, and pay a nominal fee for all design sketches. Then choose and award the commission.

- Remember that artists will not always say what you want to hear; sacred art should be judged by standards different from those applied to secular art. While such art may be a source of comfort, it may also inspire, challenge, and even disturb.

- Think how many of the great masterpieces of art have been created and preserved under the patronage of religious institutions.

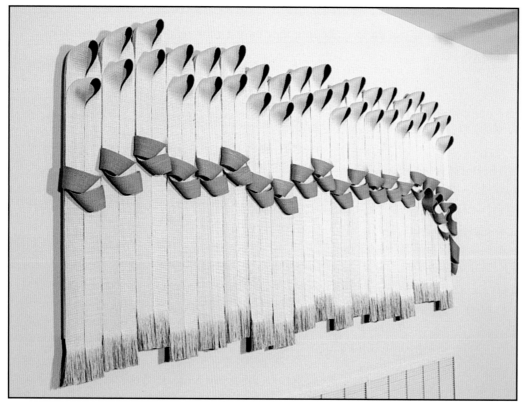

130 a, b. *"Listen to my commandments! Then shall your peace be as a river and your righteousness as the waves of the seas."* (Isaiah 48:18) by Laurie Gross, designer, and Jill Peek, weaver, Santa Barbara, California, for Congregation Albert, Albuquerque, New Mexico. 1991. 56" x 113" x 3" deep. Double weave. Linen. This sculptural piece depicts a gathering of people, symbolized by strips of cloth representing prayer shawls (tallitot). They are standing as if worshiping or singing together in community. The blue symbolizes the sea or water and functions as a common element representing the continuous chain of tradition. The piece hangs on the *bimah* (lectern) wall of the sanctuary and is a focal point for the worship environment. (Photograph by Studio 5)

131 a. (left) *Paraments* by Nancy Tiffany, Brandon, South Dakota, for St. Michael's Church, Sioux Falls. 1991. Altar cover is 37" wide with a 31" drop; pulpit fall has a 30" drop. Plain weave. Wool. Commissioned to go with Grete Bodøgaard's hangings (below). The texture of the "Tipperary Tweed" yarn complements the brick and wood of the church. Although the paraments are predominately green, other colors such as brown, tan, and blue were used to accent the colors in the tapestries. (Photographs by Jeff Viere)

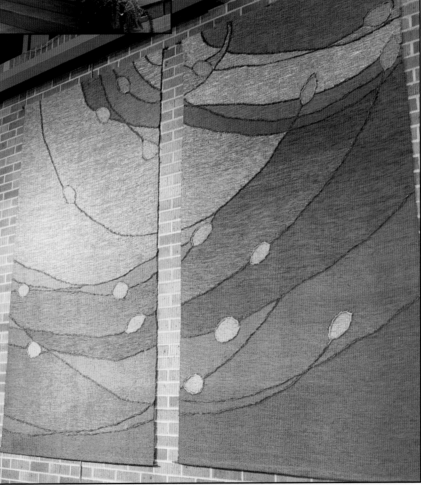

131 b. *Wall hanging* by Grete Bodøgaard, Custer, South Dakota, for St. Michael's Church, Sioux Falls. 1983. Four panels. Each 8' high x 5' wide. Plain weave with inlay. Cotton, linen, and silk with metal. This weaving was inspired by the rich, fertile soil in southeastern South Dakota where the artist lived on a farm. The design also relates to the biblical story of the seeds and where they fell. (Mark 4)

Afterword

A PERSPECTIVE

THIS BOOK IS neither the last word nor the only word about handcrafted items for Jewish and Christian worship settings. There are many other ways—besides weaving—to create *tallitot*, paraments, clergy stoles, and hangings for worship spaces. In addition, as might be expected with any subject involving American religious practices, other points of view about using weaving in worship spaces are available to the person who looks for this information.

The bibliography lists almost everything that has been written about weaving for worship, in periodical as well as book form, in this country for the past 40 or so years. Some of this material has taken the approach that any hand-woven item is appropriate for a worship setting. Other writers have set a course that is closer to the thesis of this book—that while weaving for worship may be done by anyone, it should always be done well, so as to honor God and enhance the worship environment.

It is obviously also the thesis of several of the Christian writers in this book that the current upsurge of interest in liturgical weaving began with Vatican II in 1963. The first extensive modern study of new textiles in the church was Marion Ireland's seminal work *Textile Art in the Church* (1966). This book illustrates virtually every textile technique that can be used to produce work for the church—appliqué and embroidery in addition to weaving—and virtually every form in which textiles can be used—vestments, paraments, and hangings. Ireland does not limit herself to American work but includes the Graham Sutherland tapestry at Coventry Cathedral (dedicated in 1962); many tapestries from Swedish and other European churches (some dating from the 1950s); and work by Sister Augustina Flüeler. Ireland clearly documents a movement that began before 1963—perhaps as early as the Arts and Crafts period at the beginning of the twentieth century. Vatican II legitimized this movement and gave it direction.

Ireland's point of view is that the Reformation, with its great emphasis on the Word, reduced, if it did not sever, a vital connection between visual art and worship. Her conclusion, obviously shared by many of the writers of this book, is that art is absolutely necessary to worship, for it elevates the self and takes the viewer beyond surface meaning. She warns that "When the church is divorced from art, sentimentalism rushes in." (125) Her book was important because it was the first to recognize and celebrate the fact that notable, creative, and vital modern fabric art was replacing "catalog gothic" in American churches.

The year 1975 was another important year for American weaving for worship. This was the year of *Raiment for the Lord's Service* at the Art Institute of Chicago, an exhibit of 75 chasubles owned by the Institute. It was also the year of the publication of *Weaving as an Art Form: A Personal Statement* by Theo Moorman, an English liturgical weaver. Although Moorman had been producing liturgical weaving in England for many years, her work was not widely known in this country until the publication of her book. Her book continues to be an inspiration for numerous American liturgical weavers, as shown by the large number of pieces in the Theo Moorman technique represented in this book.

All these influences, although Christian in origin, gave impetus to Judaic ritual weaving as well. Prior to the 1970s, handwoven tallitot were rare. Now, a flurry of articles in American weaving magazines covered Judaic weaving (*Shuttle Spindle & Dyepot* no. 39 [1979]; *Weaver's Journal* 6, no. 1 [1981]; *Handwoven* 5, no. 1 [1984]) Most of these articles appeared under the heading of Ecclesiastical Weaving, though the meaning of *ecclesiastical*—having to do with churches—would seem to preclude this grouping. The inclusiveness was probably a sign of the growing interest in all forms of liturgical textiles, but it was surely also a mark of the American habit of according equal space to all religious beliefs. This present book shares the same view point in its choice of title and arrangement of material, though the authors have emerged with a profound respect for the historic distinctions between the Judaic and Christian traditions of liturgical weaving—all the more striking because we have so much in common as weavers and as persons who are trying to find spiritual expression in weaving.

Even as the literature of the 1970s and 1980s rode a wave of enthusiasm for weaving for worship, many writers tried to voice the central theme of this present book: weaving for worship must be of high quality. Early in the 1980s, commentators began to express reservations about the quality of what was being produced. The same 1981 issue of *Weaver's Journal* that featured "Ecclesiastical Weaving" carried an article by Bucky King, who cautioned

> One of the unique features of weaving for the house of worship is the aesthetic ego which lures many amateurs to feel a desire to *weave something up* for their church or synagogue. (italics added)

In 1984, *Fiberarts* (September/October) ran an article decrying the lack of quality in amateur production of vestments. Patricia Malarcher quoted Charlene Burningham, a vestment maker, to sum up the unfortunate state of affairs: "So many well-meaning friends put together [vestments] with loving care and no knowledge."

Weaving historians will have to decide why the magazine coverage of liturgical weaving tapered off in 1989. Perhaps it is as Patricia Malarcher opined in *Surface Design Journal* 13, no. 3 (1989): seeing only a trickle of interest in church textiles, she cited as probable causes the pluralism of American culture, de-emphasis on ceremony, and a mutual lack of trust between artists and religious professionals. Certainly some sentiments expressed by artists interviewed for the chapter on commissions in this book suggest that many of these attitudes are still present, if not prevalent.

Nevertheless, a recent spate of books—*Art of the Spirit: Contemporary Canadian Fabric Art* by Helen Bradfield, Joan Pringle, and Judy Ridout (1992); *Patchwork Pilgrimage* by Jill Liddell (1993); and *Jewish Art* by Grace Cohen Grossman (1995)—suggest that handworkers in all faiths continue to beautify worship environments by their skills and artistic gifts, and that those skills and gifts are vital to the worship life of a community. It is impossible to say whether handcrafted items for worship are valued because they are traditional forms produced in historic ways, or new forms that have new meaning, or simply personal and unique forms—but the connection between handwork and spirituality is unequivocally established in Exodus 35:10. "All who are skillful among you shall come and make all that the Lord has commanded." This connection should be celebrated, affirmed, and confirmed by those who weave, those who commission weaving, and those who use weaving for worship. LMB

Appendices

Yarn Sizes and Setts used in *Weaving for Worship*

As we gathered the captions for this book, we asked the weavers whose work is represented to specify the yarn sizes and setts they used in their work. The following table is representative, though not exhaustive, of the answers we received. It is presented here as an aid to those who are looking for a beginning point in creating an article for use in a worship setting. Many other settings and weave structures are possible.

Yarn size	Warp sett	Weave structure
Stoles		
5/2 perle cotton	15 e.p.i.	Overshot
8/2 and 10/2 cotton	22.5 e.p.i.	Crackle
10/2 mercerized cotton	36 e.p.i.	Damask
2/18 wool	15 e.p.i.	Undulating twill
2/8 Merino wool	20 e.p.i.	Plain weave
12/2 pearle silk	24 e.p.i.	Broken twill
20/2 silk	28 e.p.i.	Twill
60/2 silk	48 e.p.i.	Tied biederwand
6/2 rayon	14 e.p.i	Monk's belt
Vestments		
5/2 cotton	16 e.p.i.	Plain weave
10/2 cotton	24 e.p.i.	Plain weave
20/2 cotton	30 e.p.1.	Crepe weave
2/12 Merino wool	20 e.p.i.	Overshot
2/18 wool/silk	30 e.p.i.	Twill
20/2 silk	34–36 e.p.i.	Twill
Paraments		
3/2 perle cotton	12 e.p.i.	Summer and winter
6/2 cotton	24 e.p.i.	Broken twill
20/2 cotton	30 e.p.1.	Crepe weave
20/2 cotton	30 e.p.i.	Overshot
10/2 mercerized cotton	36 e.p.i.	Damask
22/2 cottolin	16 e.p.i.(per layer)	Double weave pick-up
7/2 wool	12 e.p.i.	Dukagång
12/3 and 20/2 wool	18 e.p.i.	Theo Moorman technique
7/2 wool/6/2 rayon; 20/2 cotton tie-down	24 e.p.i + 12 e.p.i.	Theo Moorman technique
16/2 linen	24 e.p.i.	Plain weave
12/2 silk	18 e.p.i.	Plain weave
Palls		
6/2 rayon	10 e.p.i.	Four-harness double plain weave
20/2 silk	20 e.p.i.	Inlaid overshot
12/2 silk	30 e.p.i.	Eight-shaft crackle
Tallitot (Prayer Shawls)		
8/2 cotton	18 e.p.i.	Point twill
8/2 cotton	25 e.p.i.	Overshot
20/2 cotton	45 e.p.i.	Twill
7/2 wool	20 e.p.i.	Summer and winter
20/2 silk/wool	20 e.p.i.	Plain weave

Yarn Sizes and Setts used in *Weaving for Worship* (continued from previous page)

20/2 silk	24 + 12 e.p.i.	Theo Moorman technique
20/2 silk	36 e.p.i.	Rosepath
20/2 silk	36 e.p.i.	Twill

Temple Furnishings

5 2 wool	12 e.p.i.	Basket weave
2/24 wool	24 e.p.i.	Bronson
20/2 wool	40 e.p.i.	Double weave
16/1 linen	48 e.p.i.	Warp brocade

Tapestry

8/3 linen	10 e.p.i.	Tapestry
12/6 or 12/9 cotton	12 e.p.i.	Weft-faced tapestry
12/6 cotton	2 per cm.	Tapestry

Non-tapestry hangings

5/2 cotton	15 e.p.i.	Crackle
3-ply embroidery cotton (split)	20 e.p.i. (per layer)	Double weave pick-up
7/2 wool	10 e.p.i.	Plain weave
10/2 linen	7.5 e.p.i.	Leno
30/2 linen	15 e.p.i.	Transparency
20/2 linen	15 e.p.i.	Boundweave
16/2 linen	24 e.p.i.	False damask

Resources for Christian textile artists

JOYCE RETTSTADT
   <http://www.tiac.net/users/jrett>

HAMEL-LESAGE STUDIO
   <http://www.hlstudio.com>

THE VATICAN
   <http://www.christusrex.org>

HISTORY OF COSTUME
   <http://www.siue.edu/COSTUMES/COSTUME9_INDEX.HTML>

THE HOLY ROOD GUILD
   <http://www.holyroodguild.com>

NEEDLEWORK BOOKS
   <http://www.needleworkbooks.com/church.html>

EASTERN RITE VESTMENTS
   <http://www.the-hermes.net/~hrycak/vestment.html> (Eastern rite)

CHRISTIANS IN THE VISUAL ARTS
   Membership, P.O. Box 18117, Minneapolis, MN 55418-0117   612-378-0606

LITURGICAL ART GUILD OF OHIO
   302 Crestview Road, Columbus, OH 43202

THE GRUNEWALD GUILD
   19003 River Road, Leavenworth, WA 98826   509-763-3693

Using these patterns

The stole patterns on pages 137–139 are not life-sized. They must be enlarged so that the finished stole will be four inches wide.

1. One way to do this is to copy the design on a copier, grid it, and then copy the grid square-by-square onto a piece of paper that is the desired size to make a full-sized pattern.

2. Another way is to copy the pattern onto a transparency and then project the transparency onto a fabric or paper pattern. Simply move the projector closer or farther from the pattern paper until the outline is the desired size.

3. A third way is to use the device printed on the patterns. Enlarge the pattern until the squares are exactly one-inch square. When the squares are one-inch square, the stole patterns will be the right size—four inches across in the front. The stole patterns here need to be enlarged about 210%, so that the ten vertical squares measure ten inches. This method may require you to enlarge the enlargements several times.

Remember also that *these patterns do not include seam allowances.* Cut the fabric from ½- to ⅝-inch larger than the pattern in order to give yourself a seam allowance.

These stoles are patterns for the necklines only. The body of the stole comes straight or tapered to the desired length—about 55 inches from the center back for a person who is 5'10".

For complete construction information see the discussion in chapter 3, pages 31–33.

Drawings by Adam Brusic based on patterns by Joyce Rettstadt. Permission is granted to reproduce this pattern for personal use. Please credit *Weaving for Worship* (McMinnville, Oregon: Robin and Russ, 1998).

Curved neck for straight stole

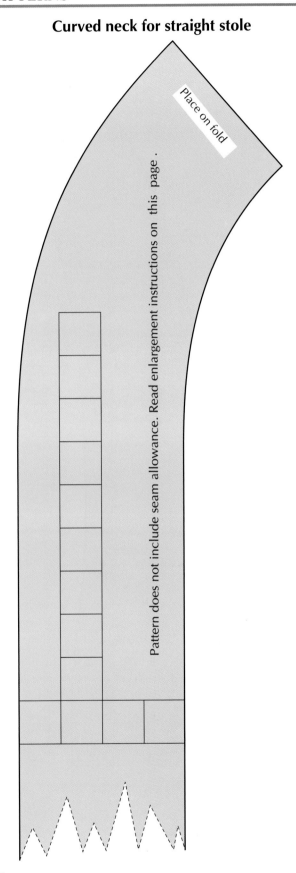

Place on fold

Pattern does not include seam allowance. Read enlargement instructions on this page.

Curved neck for tapered stole

Curved and shaped neck

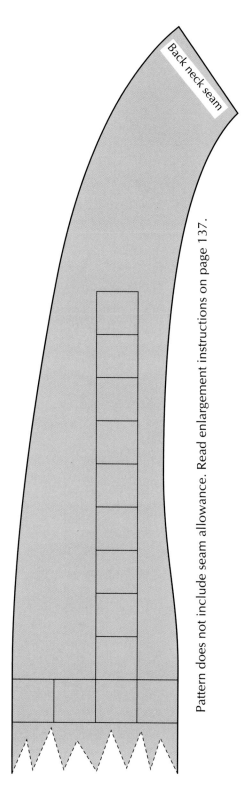

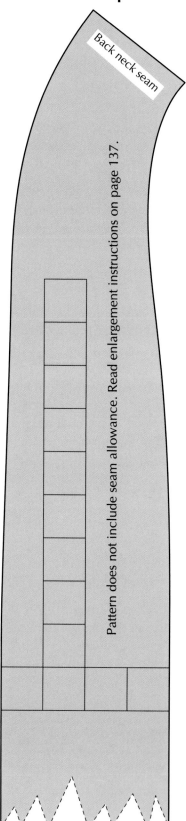

Permission is granted to reproduce these patterns for personal use. Please credit *Weaving for Worship*. (McMinnville, Oregon: Robin and Russ, 1998).

Back neck seam

Pattern does not include seam allowance. Read enlargement instructions on page 137.

Back neck seam

Pattern does not include seam allowance. Read enlargement instructions on page 137.

Back neck seam

Pattern does not include seam allowance. Read enlargement instructions on page 137.

Tapered stole

The dotted line marks the center of the stole pattern—from which the width should taper equally. Generally these stoles taper from a three-inch width at the neck to a five-inch (or other desired) width at the bottom.

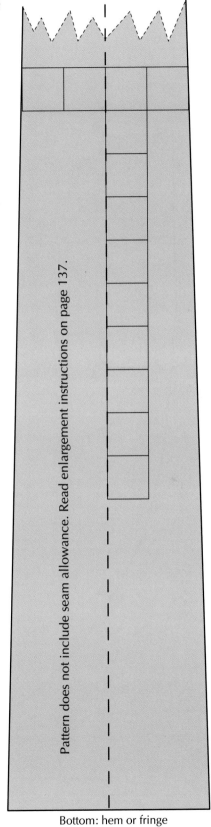

Pattern does not include seam allowance. Read enlargement instructions on page 137.

Bottom: hem or fringe

Gothic Chasuble

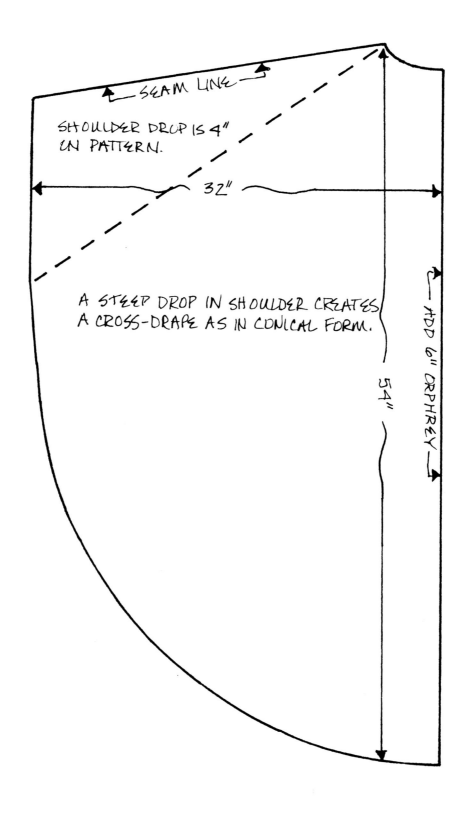

SEAM LINE

SHOULDER DROP IS 4"
ON PATTERN.

32"

A STEEP DROP IN SHOULDER CREATES
A CROSS-DRAPE AS IN CONICAL FORM.

54"

ADD 6" ORPHREY

Contemporary Chasuble

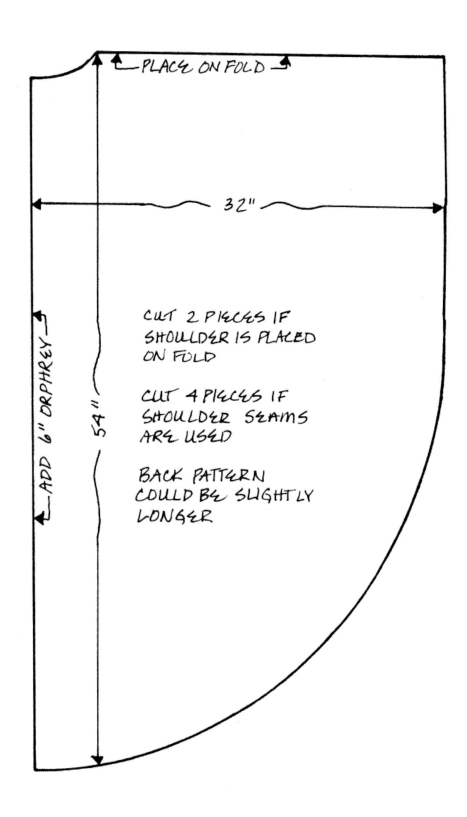

PLACE ON FOLD

32"

ADD 6" ORPHREY

54"

CUT 2 PIECES IF SHOULDER IS PLACED ON FOLD

CUT 4 PIECES IF SHOULDER SEAMS ARE USED

BACK PATTERN COULD BE SLIGHTLY LONGER

Conical Chasuble

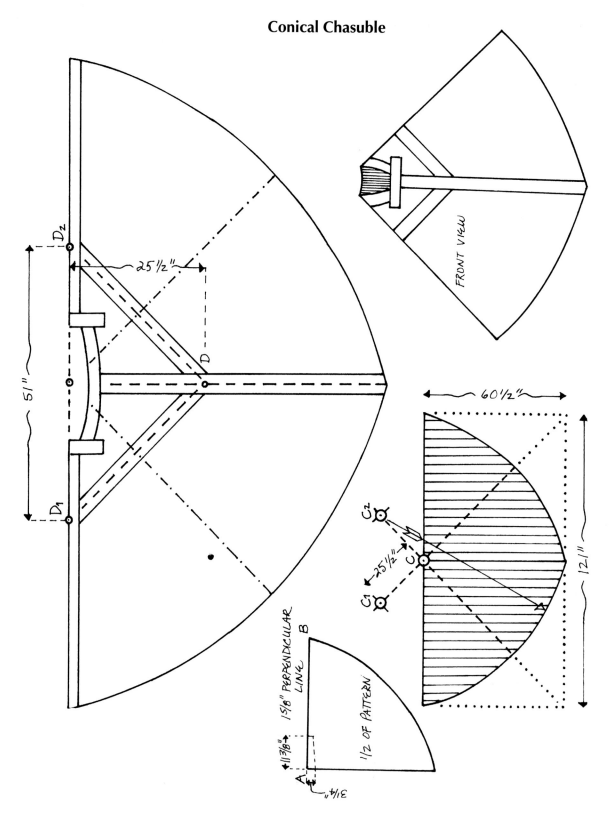

Patterns for the dalmatic, cope, and conical chasuble first appeared in issues 9, 13, and 14 of *L'ouvroir liturgique*, published by L'Abbaye of St. André, Bruges, Belgium, between 1950 and 1953.

Dalmatic

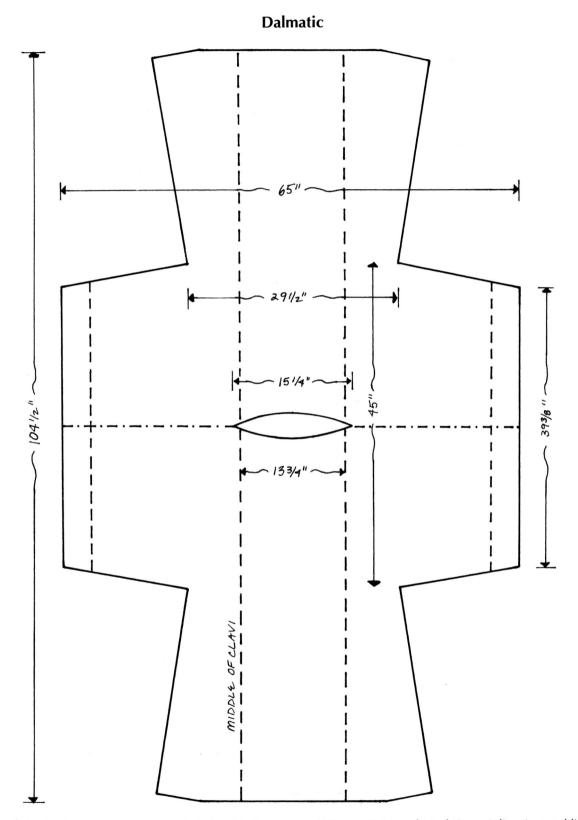

65"

29 1/2"

15 1/4"

45"

13 3/4"

104 1/2"

39 3/8"

MIDDLE OF CLAVI

Patterns for the dalmatic, cope, and conical chasuble first appeared in issues 9, 13, and 14 of *L'ouvroir liturgique*, published by L'Abbaye of St. André, Bruges, Belgium, between 1950 and 1953.

Cope

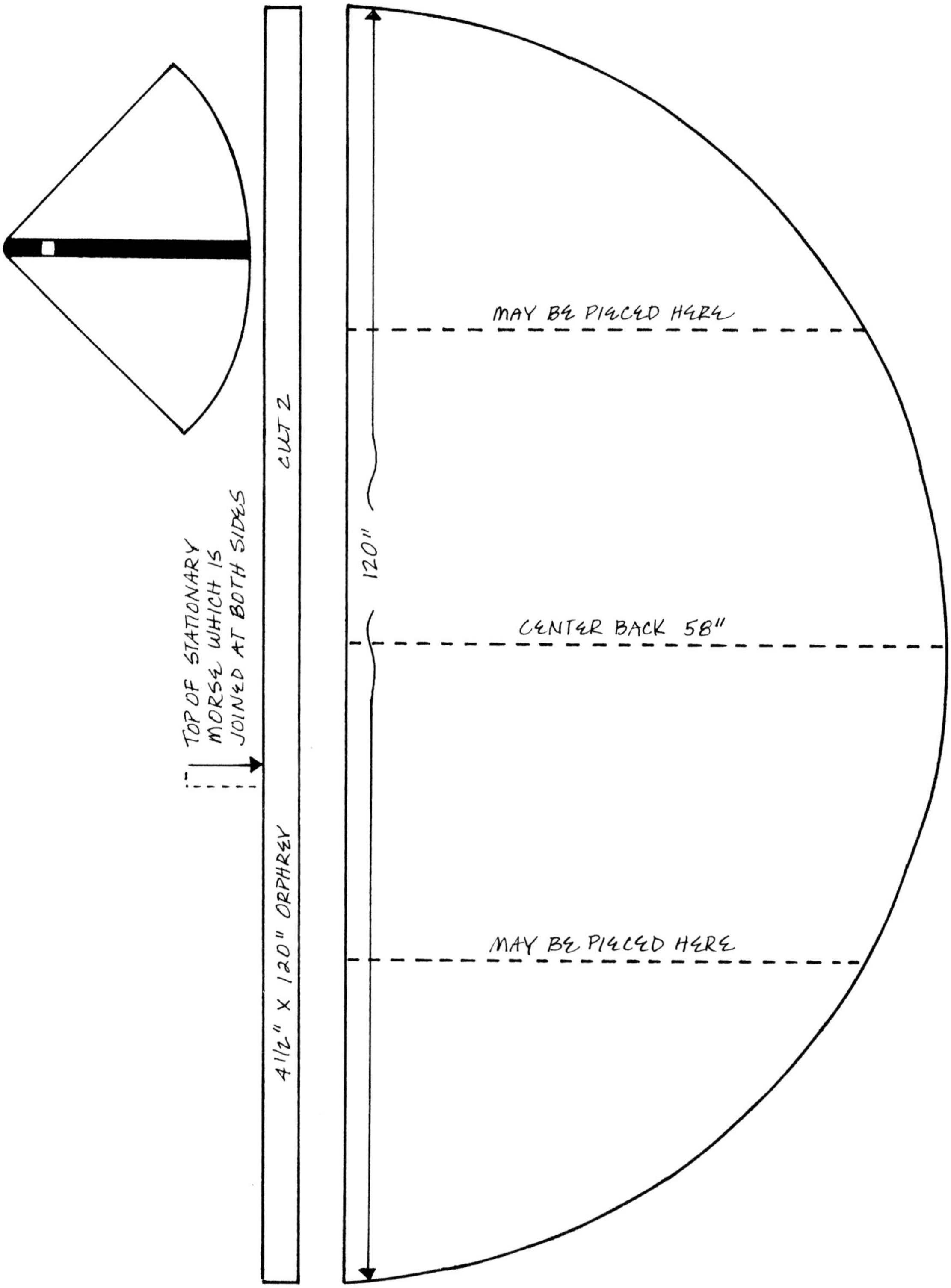
MAY BE PIECED HERE
CENTER BACK 58"
MAY BE PIECED HERE
120"
CUT 2
4 1/2" X 120" ORPHREY
TOP OF STATIONARY MORSE WHICH IS JOINED AT BOTH SIDES

Patterns for the dalmatic, cope, and conical chasuble first appeared in issues 9, 13, and 14 of *L'ouvroir liturgique*, published by L'Abbaye of St. André, Bruges, Belgium, between 1950 and 1953.

Kippah

Cut six. Pattern is shown full-sized.

Resources for Judaic textile artists

"The Tallit" Beth El Temple Center
   <http//www.shamash.org/reform/uahc/congs/ma/ma002/tallit.html>

"Tallit and Tefillin" Temple Beth Am
   <http://shamash.org/reform/uahc/congs/fl/ool/tallit.html>

Beged Ivri
   <http://www.IsraelVisit.co.il/Beged-Ivri.htn>

Needlework Books
   <http://www.needleworkbooks.com/judica.html>

American Guild of Judaic Art
   P.O. Box 1794 Murry Hill Station, New York NY 10156-0609   212-889-7581; FAX 212-779-9015

Jewish Community Center of Pittsburgh
   5738 Forbes Avenue, Box 81980, Pittsburgh PA 15217   412-521-8010; FAX 412-521-7044

Yarn

Cotton Clouds
5176 South 14th Avenue, Suite #102-HE
Safford, AZ 85546
1-800-322-7888
Cotton yarns

Crystal Palace Yarns
Dept HW90
3007 San Pablo Avenue
Berkeley, CA 94702
415-548-9988
Cotton, wool, silk, rayon

Glimåkra Looms "n" Yarns, Inc.
1338 Ross Street
Petaluma, CA 94954
1-800-829-9276
707-762-3362
Linen, cotton, cottolin, rayons, wools

Halcyon Yarns
2 School Street
Bath, ME 04530
1-800-341-0282
Cotton, wool, silk yarns

Harrisville Designs
Center Village, Box 806
Harrisville, NH 03450
603-827-3333
Shetland wool, 2-ply wool

*Henry's Attic
5 Mercury Avenue
Monroe, NY 10950
914-783-3930
Textured weft yarns

JCA, Inc.
P.O. Box 523
Townsend, MA 01469-0523
1-800-225-6340
Persian and tapestry wool in large palette

JaggerSpun
Water Street, P.O. Box 188
Springvale, ME 04083
1-800-225-8023
Fine quality wool and wool/silk yarns

Kolmes Company, Inc. (UKI)
541 W. 37th Street
New York, NY 10018
212-564-2000
Cottons

LaLame Importers
1170 Broadway
New York, NY 10006
212-921-9770
Metallic yarns

Multitex Products Corp.
54 Second Ave.
Kearny, NJ 07032
201-991-7262
Metallic tie-down gold and silver gimp

Plymouth Yarn Co., Inc.
P.O. Box 28
Bristol, PA 19007
1-800-523-8932
215-788-0459
Woolray, Doverspun, rayons

Robison-Anton Textile Company
P.O. Box 159
175 Bergen Boulevard
Fairview, NJ 07022
201-941-0500
1-800-932-0250
Cottons and embroidery floss on cones

Silk City
155 Oxford Street
Patterson, NJ 07522
201-942-1100
Wide range of yarns

The Silk Tree
Box 78
Whonnock, B.C. Canada VOM 1SO
604-687-7455
High quality silk yarns

Sunray Yarn Company, Inc.
347 Grand Street
New York, NY 10002
Order #1-800-225-6340
Wide range of yarns including rayons

Tinsel Trading Company
47 West 38th Street
New York, NY 10018
212-565-2460
Metallics

Treenway Crafts
725 Caldedonia Ave.
Victoria B.C. Canada V8T 1E4
604-383-1661
Silk, wool

Weavers Way
P.O. Box 70
Columbus, N. C. 28722
1-800-348-3483
704-894-8568
Carolina cotton, pearl cottons

Yarn Barn
918 Massachusetts
Lawrence, KS 66044
1-800-468-0035
*Pearl cottons, Shetland wools,
Doverspun, silks, variegated pearl cottons*

*Production weavers only

Equipment and supplies

Fireside Fiberarts
P.O. Box 1195 A
Port Townsend, WA 98368
360-385-7505
Tapestry looms

Leclerc Looms
P.O. Box 4
Plessisville, Quebec, Canada G6L 2Y6
819-362-2408
Upright tapestry loom

Robin and Russ Handweavers
533 North Adams St.
McMinnville, OR 97128
503-472-5760
Order # 1-800-932-8391
Looms, yarns, weaving supplies

Shannock Tapestry Looms
10402 NW 11th Ave.
Vancouver, WA 98689
206-573-7264
Looms; linen warp

Sewing Supplies

Anglo Fabrics Company, Inc.
561 Seventh Avenue, 16th floor
New York, NY 10018
212-736-2230
Beautiful fine wool fabric 60" wide

G Street Fabrics, Mail Order Service
12240 Wilkins Avenue
Rockville, MD 20852
Order # 1-800-333-9191
Will swatch fabric

Pellon
1040 Avenue of the Americas
New York, NY 10018
1-800-248-5938
Narrow rolls of pellon/case lots

Rubenstein & Ziff
1055 East 79th Street
Bloomington, MN 55420
612-854-1460
Interfacing by the bolt; Velcro® by the roll

Solo
1666 Tosca Drive
Stoughton, MA 02072
1-800-343-9670
Fax: 617-341-4705
*Ask for catalog; no color card
Waxed silamide thread for slip stitching*

Staple Sewing Aids Corporation
141 Lanza Avenue
Garfield, NJ 07026
973-546-2222

Out-of-Print Books

Hard-To-Find Needlework Books
Bette Feinstein
96 Roundwood Road
Newton, MA 02164-1217
Fax or Phone: 617-969-0942
e-mail: hardtofind@needleworkbooks.com

Tzitzit and other Judaica

Congregation Neveh Shalom
2900 SW Peaceful Lane
Portland, OR 97201
503-246-8831

The Jewish Bookstore of Greater Washington
11250 Georgia Avenue
Wheaton, MD 20902
301-942-2237

Israel Book Shop
410 Harvard Street
Brookline, MA 02368
1-800-323-7723

Reuven Praeger
Beged Ivri
111 Agripas, 2nd floor
Correspondence: PO Box 28052
Jerusalem, Israel
tel: 02-6258943
fax: 011-972-2-6255191
www.israelvisit.co.il/beged-ivri

Selected glossary of terms relating to textiles used in churches and synagogues

Alb — (also Alba, Albe, *Tunica Alba*). Eastern Orthodox: *Sticharion*. The first layer of liturgical garments in the Christian church. The alb started as the everyday wear of classical Rome — a white linen tunic with sleeves. It was ankle-length and held in place at the waist with a girdle or cincture. All ranks of clergy may wear the plain alb; it may also be worn by lay worship leaders. Historically, the alb was occasionally decorated with embroidered panels called apparels (*see*). The alb is worn under other liturgical garments.

Amice — The amice is a rectangle of fine white linen worn as a neckcloth, probably originally to protect vestments from the effects of perspiration. It is not an official part of the liturgical Christian vestments.

Antependium — An ornamental cloth to hang in front of the altar, pulpit or lectern in a church. Also called parament, fall, or frontal. It varies in color according to the season of the church year.

Apparel — A decorative embroidered panel applied to the alb or the amice. (See *alb* and *amice*.)

Ashkenazic — Pertaining to the customs and liturgy of Jews whose origins are in central and eastern Europe.

Atarah — The crown or collar of a Jewish prayer shawl (tallit). Although an *atarah* is not required, it is often used for decorative purposes. In addition, the placement of the collar indicates the right side of the garment and guides the wearer to put it on correctly. The prayer recited before putting on the tallit commonly adorns the *atarah*.

Baldachino — (also baldachin) A canopy of fabric carried in church processions or placed over an altar, throne, or dais.

Banners — May refer to any hanging textile — processional or static, semi-permanent or temporary — in a worship setting.

Bar/Bat Mitzvah — Literally means son/daughter of the commandment. A ceremony commemorating adult status in the Jewish community.

Bimah — The platform containing the raised table from which the Torah is read.

Bookmarks — Fabric strips for marking the place in processional books or service books. Sometimes used to replace a pulpit fall in a Christian church.

Burse — Part of the communion setting in certain liturgical traditions. A stiff, square fabric case (usually nine-inches square), used as a holder for the corporal and the chalice pall (*see*). The burse is usually used with a chalice veil (*see*), which it matches in color.

Cassock — A long, form-fitting black garment worn by Christian clergy and assistants, as well as by choristers and musicians.

Chalice pall — A stiffened square (usually seven-inches square) placed on the communion chalice under the veil.

Chalice veil — Used with the burse to cover the chalice before and after the Eucharist. It is usually more or less 24-inches square.

Challah cover — A cloth cover for the traditional braided bread used for the Jewish Sabbath. The challah cover is frequently embellished with the Hebrew word for Sabbath. A blessing is recited over the covered challah before it is sliced and eaten. Traditionally, two loaves are placed on the Sabbath table to commemorate the double portions of manna gathered in preparation of the Sabbath by the Israelites in the wilderness. (Exodus 16:5)

Chamsa — from the Semitic root meaning "five" — is a hand-shaped amulet worn to ward off the Evil Eye. Representing the protective hand of G-d, hand amulets have long been used in Mediterranean cultures. Often a *chamsa* has a single eye embedded in the middle of the palm to symbolize the watchful eye of G-d or to deflect the gaze of the Evil Eye. (Pronounced *hamsa*.)

Chasuble — (Also *casula, paenula*) The chasuble is the principal outer vestment used by the presiding minister celebrating the Eucharist in a Christian church. The chasuble developed from a popular traveling cloak worn in the Graeco-Roman world by both sexes and all classes. It was made from a semi-circle of woolen material with the two edges sewn together to form a conical or tent-shaped cloak, an opening being left for the head. The seam ran down the front and was usually strengthened by narrow woven bands called orphreys (*see*). The shape and form of the chasuble have varied greatly.

Chuppah—Wedding canopy. Jewish couples stand under the wedding canopy during the ceremony as a symbol of the home the new couple will establish together. This tent-like covering is usually mounted on four posts so it is freestanding; it is decorated with lettering or symbols of love and marriage.

Ciborium—a goblet-shaped container for the bread or wafers of the Eucharist.

Cincture—The belt or cord worn with the alb. (See *alb*) Can be embellished, or intricately knotted and twisted. Christian.

Clavi—Purple stripes or decorative woven or embroidered bands found on early tunics, dalmatics, and *paenulas*. Christian.

Cope—A cape worn in procession at non-Eucharistic ceremonies in place of the chasuble. It developed from an outdoor cloak worn during the latter days of the Roman Empire. It is basically a semi-circular piece of cloth held together at the front by a clasp or broad strip of cloth. (See *morse*.) Its use is not restricted to bishops and priests. As the cope became a ceremonial garment, the hood ceased to be functional and was flattened to a triangular or shield-shaped decoration at the rear of the garment. A cope frequently was, and still is, greatly decorated.

Corporal—A square piece of white linen (21 inches square or larger) upon which the chalice and the host rest during the Eucharist.

Cotta—A shortened form of surplice reaching to the waist or fingertips. It may have less fullness in the sleeves or may be sleeveless. It was often worn over the cassock by the clergy and may still be worn by members of the choir. Christian.

Credence table—a small table where the bread and the wine rest before consecration. May be covered with a credence cloth which can match the paraments. Christian.

Dalmatic—Garment worn by the deacon in a Christian church. The dalmatic and tunicle share a common origin; they are variant forms of the *alba dalmatica*. Tradition states that the basic form originated in the region of Dalmatia. It is a wide-sleeved over-garment and appears to be the garment worn by praying figures in catacomb frescoes. The earliest form was decorated by two purple *clavi* (bands).

Deacon's stole—see *stole*.

Dossal—A cloth that hangs behind the altar; usually attached to the wall; may be gathered or flat. Sometimes called a *reredos*. Christian.

Elijah's Chair—A special chair owned by a synagogue or an individual; used to lay a baby on before the circumcision ceremony. Today the chair is sometimes used for the baby-naming ceremony for girls. The tradition is based upon a legend that G-d demanded Elijah's presence at circumcisions to witness Israelites' loyalty, after the prophet complained that the Israelites were not observing their covenant. (Kings 19:10-14)

Fair linen—A (usually) linen cloth that covers the top of the altar in the Christian church. Some traditions specify five crosses—one in each corner and one in the center—to symbolize the five wounds of Christ.

Fall—see *antependium*.

Frontal—A cloth hanging that covers the entire front of the altar. Christian.

Frontlet or Superfrontal—A cloth that drops over the front of an altar by approximately 10 to 12 inches. A frontlet is sometimes used together with a full frontal. Christian.

Funeral pall—A large piece of fabric used in recent years to cover the bare casket when a funeral takes place in a church. Current custom favors white palls, although purple was once a popular color. Orphreys *(see)* may be used to cover seams.

Geneva gown—A black preaching gown (similar to an academic gown) worn by the clergy of the Reformed tradition. Christian.

G-d—Some branches of Judaism write the name of the Lord this way in order to protect the printed holy name from casual use or outright misuse. To respect these traditions, G-d has been used in glossary entries relating to Judaism.

High Holy Days—within Judaism, Yom Kippur (Day of Atonement) and Rosh Hashannah (Jewish New Year).

Humeral veil—1. A cloth or shawl covering the shoulders and hands, worn by sub-deacons when handling sacred vessels. 2. An oblong scarf worn round the shoulders at certain times during the

Mass and used in the elevation of the host to prevent contamination by the fingers of the officiating priest. Christian.

Kippah *pl. kippot* (also spelled *kepah*) — Skullcap. A head covering worn by Jews as a symbol of identity, piety, and respect. The *kippah* was traditionally worn by men, but more recently it is being worn by women as a sign of religious equality.

Lappets — Two tabs of cloth (sometimes decorated) attached to the back of a bishop's mitre.

Laudian altar cover — A parament that covers the entire altar and reaches to the floor. Christian.

Liturgical year — In the Christian church, a compression of the story of the life of Jesus and the themes of the Christian life into one calendar year (beginning with Advent and ending with Christ the King Sunday). In churches that observe the liturgical year, the colors of the paraments change according to the season that is being observed.

Maniple — A narrow strip of cloth once worn over the left arm by clerics during the Mass. It originally was a handkerchief or small towel held in the hand. By the ninth century it had developed into a vestment carried on the left forearm. It is no longer used.

Matzoh (also *matzo*) **cover** — A cloth cover used on top of the unleavened bread during Passover. This piece can also be made as a bag with three separate compartments for the matzoh referred to during the Passover service.

Mezuzah — Literally "doorpost." The mezuzah is a a piece of parchment inscribed with a specific Hebrew prayer (Deuteronomy 6:4-6 and 11:13-21). It is placed on the doorpost of a Jewish home as a symbol of identity and dedication. The word *mezuzah* is Hebrew for *doorpost* but has come to be used for both the scroll and the case.

Minyan — the minimum number of Jews — ten — that must be present to enable the lawful conduct of a public Jewish service.

Mitre — Ceremonial hat for a Christian bishop. The origin of the mitre is obscure, but it had emerged by the eleventh century as the distinctive liturgical hat of bishops. The mitre started as a simple conical cap of white linen with two lappets *(see)*. It has gone through many transformations.

Mizrach — East. A *mizrach* is a drawing, engraving, or hanging on the wall of a home indicating the direction toward Jerusalem. A Jewish worshiper faces in this direction while praying. The *mizrach* often utilizes mystical symbolism in its formulation.

Morse — The clasp or fastening device for the cope — often made of precious metals and jewels. Christian.

NRSV — New Revised Standard Version of the Bible

Opus Anglicanum — A style of English ecclesiastical embroidery lasting from the eleventh century to the end of the fifteenth, reaching its peak between 1270 and 1330. This fashion is universally esteemed for its excellence, beauty, and richness, but its use made vestments very heavy and contributed to the abbreviation of the form of the chasuble.

Orarium — The early name for a stole. In the Eastern Orthodox church it is specifically the stole of the deacon.

Ordus Romanus Primus — a document containing instructions and directions for the actual performance of each liturgical function in the Roman Catholic church. Continuously revised since the seventh century.

Orphrey — A band of woven or embroidered fabric used to decorate vestments. Orphreys may originally have been used to cover and reinforce seams. Christian.

Orthodox vestments — Orthodox vestments have undergone a parallel evolution with those of the Western Church. They differ because of rite and aesthetics, but they are basically the same garments. They developed from the same ordinary Roman dress of the first three centuries and are used on similar occasions. The biggest difference between Eastern and Western vestments is that there is no sequence of liturgical colors in the Eastern Orthodox church.

Paenula — A traveling cloak from which the chasuble is derived. The term is often used to describe the chasuble in the early period of the Christian church.

Pallium — A long woven band or scarf of white wool marked with six dark crosses, worn around the neck and shoulders with the ends hanging down in various ways, by patriarchs, archbishops, and bishops. It evolved from a much larger garment which was worn by professors and learned men in the Graeco-Roman world. It was a single piece of fabric, without seam, that was draped or folded and crossed over the left shoulder. It may be seen in the narrow version in the early Ravenna mosaics. (Eastern Orthodox: *Omophorion*)

Paraments — A generic name for any fabric hangings used on the altar, pulpit, lectern, or credence table of a church.

Parokhet (also *parochet*) — Ark curtain. The *parokhet* was originally used in the portable sanctuary in the wilderness, as described in Exodus 26. It was later used as a veil in the ancient Temple to separate the Holy of Holies from the more public ritual areas. After the destruction of the Temple, the *parokhet* was to separate the ark from the rest of the sanctuary. It still fills this function today.

Passover pillow — Passover commemorates the Exodus from Egypt. Jewish families throughout the world gather at this time of year for the festival meal known as the Seder which retells the story of the Exodus. The leader reclines on the Passover pillow. This ceremonial custom imitates the patrician manner of banqueting in Graeco-Roman times and is meant to symbolize the free status of Jews.

Purificator — A small square of linen used to wipe the lip of the chalice.

Reredos — See *dossal*.

Rochet — A vestment resembling a surplice but with tight sleeves or sleeveless. The rochet, the surplice, and the cotta developed from the alb. Christian.

Sakkos — A garment resembling the dalmatic, but worn only by the highest dignitaries. Eastern Orthodox; also *Saccos*.

Sephardic — pertaining to the customs and liturgy of Jews whose origins are in Spain and Portugal. Weaving is often more ornate than Ashkenazic pieces.

Shabbat — the seventh day or day of rest, observed sundown Friday to sundown Saturday by the Jewish faith.

Shatnez — prohibition on mixing fibers, specifically wool and linen, in tallitot or Ark curtains. (Lev. 19:19)

Sticharion — A long tunic worn by all ranks of the clergy and others involved in the ceremonies. It corresponds to the alb and is sometimes purple rather than white. Eastern Orthodox.

Stole — (also *Stola, Orarium*) A narrow strip of material worn over the shoulders in various ways as an indication of the rank of the wearer. It has been called the "yoke of Christ." The **deacon's stole** crosses over the left shoulder and joins at the right side. The stole has changed in width and length over the years. At one time the bottom was widened to a "shovel shape" to provide a larger area for decoration. Since the post-Reformation period, the stole usually matches the color sequence of the liturgical year.

Surplice — a modification of the alb; it is worn over the cassock. It is full with ample sleeves. May be worn for non-Eucharistic services and by non-clergy choristers and servers. Was originally worn over fur-lined garments and later over the cassock.

Tabernacle veil — A curtain to cover the door of the tabernacle where the reserved host (the consecrated bread) is kept in a Catholic church.

Tallit *(pl. tallitot)* — the traditional prayer shawl worn by men, and now sometimes by women, at a Jewish synagogue. The ritual fringes, called *tzitzit*, are tied in the four corners of the tallit in accordance with biblical law and serve as a reminder of all of G-d's commandments. (Exodus 20-23).

Talmud — authoritative body of Jewish tradition.

Torah mantles — The cloth covering of the Torah, the holy scroll of the Jewish people. The Torah contains the Five Books of Moses and is the basis of all Jewish law and thought. The text is handwritten on parchment and is mounted on two staves or rollers. The Torah coverings, or mantles, are made of rich textiles and adorned with silver appointments.

Tunic (also tunicle) — a shorter and plainer form of a dalmatic *(see)*. Worn by the sub-deacon but rarely used today.

Tzedakah — an act of righteousness or a good deed.

Tzitzit — ritual fringes on a tallit *(see)*.

Vestments — garments used in relation to or worn during the church service.

Bibliography

Weaving Techniques

Atwater, Mary Meigs. *Shuttlecraft Book of American Hand-Weaving*. New York: MacMillan, 1947.

Davison, Marguerite Porter. *A Handweavers Pattern Book*. Swarthmore, PA: Marguerite Davison, 1944.

Harter, Joyce and Sanders, Nadine. *Weaving that Sings*. Northfield, MN: Loomis Studio, 1994.

Heinrich, Linda. *The Magic of Linen*. Victoria, B.C., Canada: Orca Book Publishers, Ltd., 1992.

Held, Shirley. *Weaving: A Handbook for Fiber Craftsmen*. New York: Holt, Rinehart, Winston, 1973.

Jerstorp, Karin and Köhlmark, Eva. *The Textile Design Book*. Asheville, NC: Lark Books, 1988.

Moorman, Theo. *Weaving as an Art Form: A Personal Statement*. New York: Van Nostrand Reinhold, 1975.

Tidball, Harriet. *The Weaver's Book*. New York: MacMillan, 1961.

General Background

Cameron, Julia. *The Artist's Way*. New York: G. P. Putnam's Sons, 1992.

Di Sante, Carmine. *Jewish Prayer: the Origins of Christian Liturgy*. New York: Paulist Press, 1985.

L'Engle, Madeleine. *Walking on Water: Reflections on Faith & Art*. Wheaton, IL: Shaw, 1980.

History of Christian Vestments

Clothed in Majesty: European Ecclesiastical Textiles from the Detroit Institute of Arts. Detroit: Founder's Society, 1991.

Exhibition of Liturgical Arts, 41st International Eucharistic Congress, 1976. Exhibition catalog.

Grabar, Andre. *Early Christian Art*. New York: Odyssey Press, 1968.

Mayo, Janet. *A History of Ecclesiastical Dress*. New York: Holmes & Meier Publishers, Inc., 1984.

Meyer-Thurman, Christa C. *Raiment for The Lord's Service: A Thousand Years Of Western Vestments*. Chicago: Art Institute of Chicago, 1975.

Norris, Herbert. *Church Vestments: Their Origin and Development*. New York: E.P. Dutton and Co., 1950.

Pocknee, C.E. *Liturgical Vesture, Its Origins And Development*. Westminster, MD: The Canterbury Press, 1961.

Roulin, Dom E. A. *Vestment and Vesture*, translated by Dom Justin McCann, O.S.B., Westminster, MD: Newman, 1950.

Volbach, Wolfgang Fritz. *Early Christian Art*. New York: Harry N. Abrams, Inc., 1965.

Weitzmann, Kurt, et al. *The Icon*. New York: Knopf, 1982.

Christian Symbolism

Caemmerer, Richard R., Jr. *Visual Art in the Life of the Church*. Minneapolis: Augsburg Press, 1983.

Cooper, J.C. *An Illustrated Encyclopedia of Traditional Symbols*. New York: Thames and Hudson, 1979.

Eliade, Mircea. *Symbolism: the Sacred and the Arts*. New York: The Continuum, 1992.

Ferguson, George. *Signs and Symbols in Christian Art*. New York: Oxford University Press, 1954. Reprinted 1974.

Contemporary Christian Textiles

Besse, Pat. *Embroidery for the Church*. Newton Centre, MA: Charles Branford Co., 1975.

Bishop's Committee on the Liturgy. Environment and Art in Catholic Worship. Washington, D.C.: National Conference of Catholic Bishops, 1978.

Blair, M.C. and Ryan, C. *Banners And Flags*. New York: Harcourt Brace Jovanovich, 1977.

Helen Bradfield, Joan Pringle, Judy Ridout. *Art of the Spirit, Contemporary Canadian Fabric Art*. Toronto & Oxford: Dundurn Press, 1992.

Dean, Beryl. *Church Needlework*. London: B.T. Batsford, 1961.

Dean, Beryl. *Designing Ecclesiastical Stitched Textiles*. Kent: Search Press Ltd, 1993.

Dean, Beryl. *Embroidery in Religion and Ceremonial*. London: B.T. Batsford, 1981.

Dean, Beryl. *Ideas for Church Embroidery*. London: B.T. Batsford, 1968.

Ireland, Marion P. *Textile Art in the Church*. New York: Abingdon Press, 1966.

King, Bucky & Martin, Jude. *Ecclesiastical Crafts*. New York: Van Nostrand Reinhold Co., 1978.

Liddell, Jill. *The Patchwork Pilgrimage*. New York: Penguin Books USA, Inc., 1993.

Welch, Nancy. *Tassels*. Asheville, NC: Lark Books, 1992.

Selected articles on weaving for Christian settings

Austin, Carole. "Early Christian Church Curtain" *Fiber Arts* 14, no. 2. (1987): 28.

Brusic, Lucy. "From the 'Crooked Parament' to the 'Thread of living memory'" *Arts* 9, no. 1 (1997): 4.

Centner, The Rev. David J., O.C.D. "Reflections on the Chasuble," *Handwoven* 5, no. 1 (1984): 36.

Centner, The Rev. David J., O.C. D. "The Living Thread of Memory," *Handwoven* 10, no. 1 (1989): 45.

Corlin, Eva. "Textile Art in Uppsala Cathedral," *Väv* 2 (1984).

Craeger, Clara. "The Corporate Commission," *Shuttle, Spindle & Dyepot*, no. 61 (winter 1984): 38.

Droege, Carol. "An Advent Chasuble," *Shuttle Spindle & Dyepot*, no. 65 (1985).

Drooker, Penelope B. "The Making of a Weaver," *Shuttle Spindle & Dyepot*, no. 55 (summer 1983): 28.

Duvosin, Mrs. Charles. "Pure Silk Ecclesiastical Vestments," *Shuttle Spindle & Dyepot*, no. 13 (winter 1972): 16.

Grewenow, Melissa Coe. "Visual Sermons" *Shuttle Spindle & Dyepot*, no. 108, (fall 1996): 48.

Hahn, Roslyn J. "Weaving for the Church—A Challenge!" *Handwoven* 5, no. 1 (1984): 32.

Hahn, Roslyn. "Violet Vestment," *The Weaver's Journal* 8, no. 3 (1983-84).

Harvey, Nancy. "A special piece—A special place," *The Weaver's Journal* 8, no. 1 (1983).

Jensen, Netty. "Vestment Variations," *The Weaver's Journal* 10, no. 3 (1986).

King, Bucky. "Ecclesiastical Weaving," *The Weaver's Journal* 4, no. 1 (1981): 35.

Lockwood, Dianne. "The Ecclesiastical Weaving of Dianne Lockwood," *The Weaver's Journal* 4, no. 3. (1980).

Lockwood, Dianne. "Symbolic or sacred—A personal view," *The Weaver's Journal* 9, no. 3. (winter 1985).

Malarcher, Patricia. "The Liturgical Vestment: A Contemporary Overview," *Fiber Arts* 11, no. 5 (1984): 58.

Malloy, Kim, OSB. "The Eucharistic Vestments," *The Weaver's Journal* 4, no. 1 (1981): 37.

McIntosh, Joan W. "Open Weave Altar Hangings, "*Shuttle Spindle & Dyepot*, no. 14 (spring, 1973): 15.

Murphy, Mathilda. "Green and White Church Paraments in Crackle," *Shuttle Spindle & Dyepot*, no. 19 (summer 1974): 54

Paul, Jan. "Weaving Works for Worship," *The Weaver's Journal* 4, no. 1 (1981): 40.

Reed, Kathy. "Stoles and Chasubles," *The Weaver's Journal* 4, no. 1 (1981): 46.

Ridgeway, Terese. "Stepping Out," *Shuttle Spindle & Dyepot*, no. 69 (winter 1986): 83.

Rizner, Constance B. "Seasonal Stoles," *Shuttle Spindle & Dyepot*, no. 70 (spring 1987): 22.

Rodman, Terry. "Liturgical Weaving," *Handwoven* 10, no. 1 (1989): 50.

Temple, Mary. "Traditional Dukagång for Contemporary Textiles," *Handwoven* 8, no. 3 (1987): 57.

"Thanks and Praise—The New Spirituality," *Surface Design* 12, no. 3 (1989). Entire issue.

Tidball, Harriet. "Fair linens for the church," *Shuttlecraft*, March 1958.

Ziemke, Dene. "Ecclesiastical Weaving, Part 1," *Shuttle Spindle & Dyepot*, no. 35 (summer 1978): 31.

Ziemke, Dene. "Ecclesiastical Weaving, Part 2," *Shuttle Spindle & Dyepot*, no. 36 (fall 1978): 42.

Ziemke, Dene. "Ecclesiastical Weaving, Part 3," *Shuttle Spindle & Dyepot*, no. 37 (winter 1978): 46.

Zimmer, Barbara. "Ecclesiastical Weaving for Easter," *Heddle*, March 1988.

Jewish Ceremonial Art

Aber, Ita. *The Art of Judaic Needlework.* New York: Charles Scribner's Sons, 1979.

Eis, Ruth. *Ornamented Bags for tallit and tefillin.* Berkeley: The Judah L. Magnes Museum, 1984.

Frankel, Ellen and Teutsch, Betsy Platkin. *The Encyclopedia of Jewish Symbols.* Northvale, N.J.: Jason Aronson Inc., 1992.

Frazier, Nancy. *Jewish Museums of North America.* New York: John Wiley & Sons, Inc., 1992.

Grossman, Grace Cohen. *Jewish Art.* China: Hugh Lauter Levin Associates, Inc., 1995.

Idelsohn, Abraham. *Ceremonies of Judaism.* Cincinnati: National Federation of Temple Brotherhoods, 1930.

Ina Golub: The Work of the Weaver in Colors. New York: Ina Golub and Yeshiva University: 1996.

Kampf, Avram. *Contemporary Synagogue Art. Developments in the United States, 1946-1964.* New York: Union of American Hebrew Congregations, 1966.

Kaplan, Aryeh. *Tzitzith Thread of Light.* New York: National Conference of Synagogue Youth, 1984.

Milgrom, Jo. *Handmade Midrash: Workshops in Visual Theology.* Philadelphia: The Jewish Publication Society, 1992.

Rockland, Mae Shafter. *The Work of Our Hands.* New York: Schocken Books, 1973.

Salamon, Kathryn. *Jewish Ceremonial Embroideries.* London: B.T. Batsford, 1988.

Siegel, Richard; Strassfield, Michael; Strassfield, Sharon. *The Jewish Catalog.* Philadelphia: The Jewish Publication Society of America, 1973.

Springer, Selma and Friends. *Designs of Judaica.* Santa Monica, CA: Simcha, 1986.

Reference

Hertz, Dr. J. H. *Pentateuch & Haftorahs.* London: Soncino Press, 1981.

"Textiles." *Encyclopedia Judaica,* vol. 15, 1036-1043. Encyclopedia Judaica Jerusalem: The MacMillan Company, 1971.

"Tallit." *Encyclopedia Judaica,* vol. 15, 743-746. Encyclopedia Judaica Jerusalem: The MacMillan Company, 1971.

Selected articles about Judaic weaving

Bercey, Lee. "Prayer Shawls," *Handweaver & Craftsman,* winter 1969.

"Draperies for a Synagogue," *Handweaver & Craftsman,* fall 1967.

Fireside, Bryna. "Shawl of Freedom," *Hadassah Magazine,* January 1984.

Furniss, Frances. "Laurie Herrick, Contemporary Weaver & Teacher," *Handweaver & Craftsman,* fall 1967.

Golub, Ina. "Tapestries at Temple Emanu-El," *Shuttle Spindle & Dyepot* no. 53 (winter 1982): 41.

"Hortense Amram, Designer and Weaver of Ceremonial Textiles," *Handweaver & Craftsman,* fall 1958.

"Jewish Ceremonial Textiles," *Handweaver & Craftsman,* fall 1956.

Johnson, Faye. "Jewish Textiles," *Handwoven:* 5, no. 1 (1984): 35.

Johnson, Faye. "Tallit," *Handwoven* 5, no. 1 (1984): 91.

Kantor, Phyllis. "The Work of the Weaver in Colors," *Handwoven* 10, no. 1 (1989): 55.

Kleinman, Susan "Undercover Art," *Hadassah Magazine,* January 1989.

Lebbovitch, Constance. "Design for Torah Cover," *Shuttle Spindle & Dyepot* no. 16 (fall 1973): 18.

Longard, Evelyn. "Weaving for the Synagogue," *Shuttlecraft,* March 1959.

McCrosky, Judy. "Weaving Jewish Tradition," *Shuttle Spindle & Dyepot* no. 74 (spring 1988): 30.

Rapp, Sylvia. "Temple Tapestry," *Shuttle Spindle & Dyepot* no. 58 (spring 1984): 24.

Reisner, Neil. "Shawl of Fame,"*Hadassah Magazine,* January 1984.

Renee, Paula. "Tree Of Life: A commission for the Jewish Chapel at West Point," *Shuttle Spindle & Dyepot* no. 66 (spring 1986): 80.

Skydell, Ceil. "Under Cover," *Hadassah Magazine,* October 1993.

Sofer, Tamar. "From the Closets of Antiquity," *Hadassah Magazine,* January 1989.

Sylvan, Katherine."A Tale of a Tallis." *The Weaver's Journal* 6, no. 1 (1981): 42.

Ziemke, Dene. "Ecclesiastical Weaving, Part 4," *Shuttle Spindle & Dyepot,* no. 38 (spring1978): 65.

Tapestry weaving

Beutlich, Tadek. *The Technique of Woven Tapestry.* New York: Watson-Guptill, 1967.

Brostoff, Lata. *Weaving a Tapestry.* (Loveland, Colorado: Interweave Press, 1982.

Francis, Kathy and Wellnitz, Susan. "Hanging Methods that Work and Last," *Shuttle Spindle & Dyepot,* no. 98, (spring 1994): 14.

Harvey, Nancy. *Tapestry Weaving: A Comprehensive Study Guide.* Loveland, Colorado: Interweave Press, 1991.

Harvey, Nancy. *Tapestry Weaving-Level I (A Video Workshop).* Colfax, CA: Victorian Video Productions, 1985.

Harvey, Nancy. *Tapestry Weaving-Level II (A Video Workshop).* Colfax, CA: Victorian Video Productions, 1987.

Pearson, Alec. *The Complete Book of Tapestry Weaving.* New York: St. Martin's Press, 1984.

Redman, Jane. *Frame Loom Weaving.* New York: Van Nostrand Reinhold, 1976.

Russell, Carol. *The Tapestry Handbook.* Asheville, N.C.: Lark Books, 1975.

Swanson, Karen. *Rigid Heddle Weaving.* New York: Watson-Guptill, 1975.

Business Practices

Dillehay, James. *Weaving Profits: How to Make Money Selling Your Handwovens or Any Other Crafts.* Torreon, NM: 1993.

INDEX

An *italicized entry is a plate. Every work by every artist is indexed by the artist's name. However, to conserve space, plates of vestments, stoles, tallits, and paraments are indexed as such only when they appear apart from the chapter in which they are discussed. Thus, stoles that appear within chapter 3 (The Liturgical Stole) are not indexed below.*

MARJORIE FORD, owner of Cantraip Studio, has been creating handwoven art fabrics, tapestries, and liturgical textiles for churches and synagogues throughout the country for over 35 years. Educated at Brown University and Pratt Institute in the liberal arts and industrial design, Ford has taught seminars for national conferences of the Handweavers Guild of America, the Midwest Weavers' Conference, the American Lutheran Church, the Evangelical Lutheran Church in America, the American Guild of Organists, and other groups interested in the arts and liturgy. Her work has been published in *Shuttle Spindle and Dyepot, Fiber Arts, Handwoven, Your Church, The Lutheran Bond,* and *Faith and Form,* and has won awards from the Midwest Weavers' Conference and the Guild for Religious Architecture. She lives in Minneapolis, Minnesota.

LUCY BRUSIC is an editor and writer who is also a weaver. She learned to weave in Ithaca, New York, from Marjorie Ruth Ross and has been weaving for more than 25 years. She specializes in the crackle weave—in both ecclesiastical and non-ecclesiastical uses. Her weaving has won prizes at the New England Weavers' Seminar. She is the author or editor of four previous books, including *Weaving that Sings* by Joyce Harter and Nadine Sanders. She lives in St. Paul, Minnesota.

JOYCE RETTSTADT studied Textile Design at Moore College of Art in Philadelphia, Pennsylvania, and then began weaving in 1968. Upon graduation with a M.A. from Clark University in 1979 with an M.A. thesis entitled, "History of the Chasuble in the Christian Church," she began her own single-artist studio focusing exclusively upon custom, handwoven vestments and paraments. Completed liturgical commissions may be seen in 40 states and abroad. Her vestments have been exhibited nationally at Convergences (sponsored by HGA), and her work has been accepted repeatedly at the Liturgical Art Guild of Ohio's biennial juried exhibit. Reproductions of completed commissions have appeared in several journals including *Handwoven, Modern Liturgy,* and *Environment & Art.* Completed commissions include an installation in the Marquand Chapel at Yale Divinity School, New Haven, Connecticut. She lives in Princeton, Massachusetts.

Artists and partners of Hamel-LeSage Studio, **MARC HAMEL** and **ED LESAGE,** have been handweavers for some 20 years. Mr. Hamel is a graduate of the University of Notre Dame with a degree in Theology and a concentration in Medieval studies. Mr. LeSage is a graduate of St. John's Seminary with a Master of Divinity. Both are former Trappist monks who first learned their craft while in the monastery and have been perfecting, and addicted to, it ever since. The monastery is also where they began their work with vesture design and tailoring. Mr. Hamel did his weaving apprenticeship with Ms. Carol Markarian. Mr. LeSage apprenticed under Mr. Hamel. In subsequent years further study and consultation was done with Joyce S. Rettstadt. Hamel-LeSage Studio is located in Barre, Massachusetts.

JOYCE HARTER began weaving in 1971. Her husband is a Lutheran clergyman and her first commissions were stoles for him. For the first three years she experimented with various weaving methods, but when she discovered the Theo Moorman technique in 1975, she knew that this method of weaving would permit her to use her background in the visual arts. Under the business name, Joyce Harter Weavers, Joyce designed and wove over 500 stoles, 200 sets of paraments, and over 100 wall hangings in the Theo Moorman technique. Her work is in use in churches in 26 states and several foreign countries. She sold her business in 1993. Joyce has taught the Theo Moorman technique at HGA Convergences and has exhibited at many regional conferences. Published works include *Untying the Warping Problem* (Loomis Studios: 1993) and *Weaving that Sings* (with Nadine Sanders) (Loomis Studios: 1995). She lives in Northfield, Minnesota.

PAULA STEWART is currently producing commissioned liturgical work for private individuals as well as public spaces. She has a bachelors degree in Fine Arts from the University of Massachusetts and attended Pratt Institute in New York for graduate work. She has studied weaving with national and international instructors. Her participation in local Northwest shows and international exhibits has brought her well-deserved recognition for her work as a fiber artist. She lives in Portland, Oregon.

JEANETTE MACMILLAN PRUISS is a native Cincinnatian, receiving her B.A. from Edgecliff College. Having learned to weave 36 years ago at the Cincinnati Art Museum under Hazel Walters Keethler, she has been commissioned to weave hangings, tapestries, and liturgical textiles in Ohio, Indiana, and Pennsylvania. Jeanette was a founding partner in Peach Tree Studio, a weaving, spinning, and knitting shop in Madeira, Ohio, and taught textile arts for 21 years at Edgecliffe College. She has had exhibitions in Ohio, Kentucky, and Texas and her work is in many private collections. She lives in Terrace Park, Ohio.